poems: sonnets, lyrics
and the like

O
r
a
l

poems: sonnets, lyrics
and the like

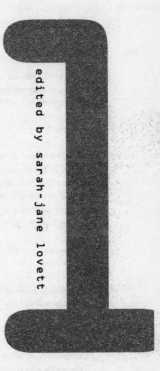

edited by sarah-jane lovett

S

SCEPTRE

First published in 1999 by Hodder and Stoughton
A division of Hodder Headline
A Sceptre Paperback

British Library CIP catalogue record for this title
is available from the British Library

ISBN 0 340 75051 0

Designed by Peter Ward
Typeset by Hewer Text Ltd, Edinburgh
Printed and bound in Great Britain by
Caledonian Book Manufacturing, Glasgow

Hodder and Stoughton
A division of Hodder Headline
338 Euston Road
London NW1 3BH

Dedicated to Otis **and** Queenie Ingrams

Thanks to: Lovett family; **Ingrams family;** Lisa Moylett; **Sarah Such;** Carole Welch; **Sarah Ballard;** Gerry O'Boyle; Patrick Moylett; **Kate Chancellor;** Jan Woroniecki; **David Sexton; Mr Bryson;** Dave Bedford; Jaffa; Rodent; **Joe Cairo; Guy Kennaway;** Sam Taylor-Wood; **Big Al;** Alasdair Oliver; Chris Briggs; **T.C.;** Andrew McAllister; **Sebastian Shakespeare;** Victoria Clarke; **Georgina Coombs;** Stuart Staples; Liam Carson; **Jem Rolls;** Kate; Sean.

Contents

Introduction

Oh how we hate poetry
Its grim little lines
Sitting all smug on the page
Poignant and self-important,
Watery statements
Of the elements and nature
Or free verse falling like
Grey gloomy sleet
Stop.

Poetry often suffers most from its oppressive title. Unlike its more glamorous bedfellow 'Art', which seems open, innovative and contemporary, for many people 'Poetry' conjures images of trying to stay awake through tedious, self-important outpourings. Yet in the last five years or so, we have seen a huge resurgence of interest in and rediscovery of the spoken word and its potential. The remarkable number of people performing poetry throughout the country, the range, depth and vitality of expression, the sheer diversity of style and content; all of this demands attention, insists on being heard. Whether in short, long, loving, funny, sad, bitter, sick, strange or surreal form, whether anecdotal, confessional or allegorical, people everywhere are talking, shouting, reciting, rapping, blurting, singing and this surely enriches our lives.

This expansion is partly the result of ad hoc mixing of the spoken word with other genres, a cross fertilisation which has resulted in poets performing across Britain, Ireland, and Europe, at music festivals such as Glastonbury and T In The Park, private views and raves, and as well as supporting major bands.

The influence and importance of contemporary icons such as Nick Cave, P.J. Harvey and Shane MacGowan in all this must be acknowledged. These are artists whose words matter to masses of people. Their songs are anthems to many and are listened to intently, memorised, analysed and ultimately embraced. Pop stars such as Jarvis Cocker and Nicky Wire create truthful and evocative scenarios which are capable of elevating the simple pop song to a more sophisticated, provocative and fundamentally word based level. Spoken word is married to sculpted sound by Stuart David of Belle and Sebastian, David Boulter of The Tindersticks, and Aidan Moffat and Malcolm Middleton of Arab Strap in a union that defies classification. By the same token, many poets included here such as Jock Scot, Fay Hart, Lloyd Evans to name but a few are, in my mind, breaking new ground, and are excelling in their idiosyncratic storytelling. They remain surprisingly unknown outside a certain clique. This book aims to change that.

This anthology is an attempt to reflect the urgency and vitality that abounds in poetry and lyrics today. It makes no claim to be definitive, or exclusive. It is representative. Call what's collected here performance poetry, spoken word, street rap or stand up. Call it what you will. The terms are inadequate, the work far from it.

Whether in future this group of writers will be named the hysterics, neurotics, psychotics, or simply alcoholics with a taste for recreational substances remains to be seen. While any selection process is, of necessity, subjective, it has been in some ways difficult, not because of the lack of decent material, but the wealth of it, like tapping into a very rich seam. In other ways, however it has been easy, for the pieces chosen stood out like fabulous paintings. What I believe they share, and what I sought to bring together, is an honesty of expression and a willingness to confront the un-tarted-up realities of life. There is nothing effete here. I have excluded the lunatic fringe and chosen contributors who focus on the eternal themes. I wanted to produce a book not for anoraks, but a book that is accessible, available, up front and open to all.

Most of the pieces present snapshots of life, portraying a mood or a perspective often pertinent to the class, education and background of the author. Much of the writing is frank, shocking and stark, some very experimental. Some is word salad, seemingly erratically tossed together. Much of the writing is in the vernacular, Trainspotting-speak, argot. Some of it is written in character. Some makes us feel uncomfortable through its honesty and lack of artifice or the painful experiences addressed. Yet where there are struggles with addiction, alienation, obsession and regret alongside social comment and concern, there is also hope, the pursuit of happiness, love and humour.

The immediacy of this work can be extremely arresting in performance, sometimes intimate and confidential, at other times bold and brash. Either way it has an element of 'punk'. The core lesson I have learnt from what I have seen, heard and received is that language is alive and well. In performance it constantly grows and evolves, making sound and shape and evoking mood. For those weaned on reading the likes of the romantics and metaphysical poets this is a new dawning.

I am indebted to the artists involved here for their amazing enthusiasm and generosity in making their work available for this original anthology, some previously withheld from publication and some especially written for inclusion. Some of it has been produced before in self published books, some in periodicals, journals, newspapers and even on the internet.

Performance poetry may at times be strident and abrasive, it is not always pretty or PC. In many ways it can be seen as our own brand of 'dirty realism'. The telling it the way it really is. What therefore must be acknowledged is its existence. And it's Oral. As Van Morrison so succinctly put it – Rave on John Donne!

London, 1999

From Hamburg to Jo'burg, Oslo to Soho, **Patience Agbabi** has catapulted poetry into the '90s. She won the 1997 Excelle Literary Award for Poetry and is a member of the LAB Literature Advisory Group. She's inspired by '90s poetry, '80s rap and '70s disco. In her first collection, *R.A.W.* (Rhythm and Word), street and élite meet in 'forms that range from rap to iambic pentameter to concrete poetry'. Her second collection, *Transformatrix*, is being published by Payback Press in Spring 2000.

E (Manic Dance Mix A)

Turn on tune in
pop till you drop
you can't stop
pass go merry-go
happy-go human
relay race pace
bomb the bass
Ban the Bill
pop that pill
rave love-slave
pop your powdery
rose-hip pound
while time rolls
gold and round
60s theme 90s hit
6 and 9 in orbit
if you can't beat it
eat it if you can't
mellow sell out
6+9 flip Pisces trip
Aquarius is hip
so spit out the pip

DJ G.O.D. this is DJ G.O.D.
Creator of the Heaven and the E
Your manic MC M D M A
Director of L O V E

Hippyhippyhippyhippy
yippyippyippyippy
yuppy yuppi yuppie

Let there be lasers let there be
man made man made man
made man in my own image
free market enterprise LOVE
fruit of the factorytorytreetree

It's Better Post- than Pre-

I'm sitting on this toilet seat
I'm reading graffiti
and some of it's political
and some of it is cheeky
but I only see red
coz I'm feeling rather freaky
when it comes to having PMT
no woman can beat me
I'm speedy   I'm angry
I'm horny   I'm stoned
I want to be touched
and I WANNA BE LEFT ALONE
PMT I pick my target
PMT I start to load
PMT I pull my trigger
my tits are ready to explode

Stick em on   stick em in   stick em up gals
stick em on   stick em in   stick em up
if you wanna shoot an arrow
then it's time to load your barrel
stick em on   stick em in   stick em up

I remember that first memory
a dark red stain
I didn't feel no nausea
I didn't feel no pain
I was a woman   a warrior
erotic   arcane
and once a month a lunatic

in nappies and insane
My mum she bought the towels in
she didn't make a fuss
she told me about men
and she said 'It's them and us'
mini   regular
Super   SUPER PLUS
I stuck em on   I stuck em in
and then I stuck em up

Stick em on   stick em in   stick em up gals
stick em on   stick em in   stick em up
if you wanna sate your lust
then insert a Super Plus
stick em on   stick em in   stick em up

Remember waiting in the queue
to pay for that first pack
you're looking at the ceiling
with your hands behind your back
then it's you and the assistant
who's since got the sack
says 'DOCTOR WHITE'S MINI PRESS-ON TOWELS
how much are they Jack?'
Or you're sitting on the toilet seat
one hand between your thighs
the other with instructions
on how to DIY
you hop skip and jump about
you ought to win a prize
and your entire extended family
are queuing up outside

Stick em on   stick em in   stick em up gals
stick em on   stick em in   stick em up
if you're paranoid in public
I can't find a better subject
stick em on   stick em in   stick em up

They have adverts on the telly
to say they are discreet
disposable   collapsible
invisible   and neat
the ones that make you sit as if
you're one of the élite

and ones that give you ATTITUDE
when walking down the street
The ones that won't go down the loo
however much you try
that bloated towel or tampon
that simply will not die
and some that leak and some you like
and they're the ones you by
if you're cool rosé is quite passé
you stick to extra-dry

Stick em on   stick em in   stick em up gals
stick em on   stick em in   stick em up
if you're thinking of your image
then forget about your spillage
stick em on   stick em in   stick em up

Well some call it PMS
and some call it PMT

some say it's a deficiency
of vitamin B
some say it is a myth
some say it is reality
but those of us who have it know
it's better post-   than pre-
some call it The Curse
from the story of Creation
the Time of the Month
or just menstruation
for the past   the present
and the future generation
I think it's time we gave ourselves
a STANDING OVULATION

Stick em on   stick em in   stick em up gals
stick em on   stick em in   stick em up
if you're paranoid in public
I can't find a better subject
stick em on   stick em in   stick em up

Rich Beale is vocalist on all Head, Receiver and Pregnant records. He regularly exhibits his drawings and is currently working on three new LPs and a short biography of Bernard de Ventadour.

John XXVIII

Your father was an object of my detestation
As an emissary of the devil
So I took a ride to visit him
Across the Western Levels

Past a pebbled rocky prominence
All covered with roots and herbs and shrubs
Like Palestine

And a Mediterranean landscape
With rocky towers
All split and cracked that I might climb

And I met a Jew named Greville
And an atheist named John and
The train was really full
Because some hawklords had got on

I found him high above the hedgerows
Alive and well and stoned and drunk and fine
And your father was no object of my detestation
As I casted out my devil
With this rhyme

Blindworms

It's like singers
They're sick of singing sixty f***ing songs
For about six f***ing quid
In some stupid f***ing club, in Manchester
Sixty stupid f***ing songs
For about six f***ing quid
In some stupid club

Bobby
As he falls down on a very muddy knee and says to me
O Bobby can you hear
The music of a very muddy Blindworm?

A musical Monody
To the white disc that represents his professional playing
    career

Go Bobby go, Down to Mexico
But can you hear the music of the Blindworms?

It's like football
Have you seen Rocastle's monstrous facial spasms?
I dreamt he were playing wearing an Easter bonnet
Osgood
Peter Osgood
Unrecognisable, bloated, all blue and damp

As they say in Germany
'Jedermann sein eigner fussball' (sic)

Rich Beale

I think Bobby should be allowed to express his feelings
Even if it is in a Northern accent
Bobby, thou shalt not steal Bobby
Go Bobby go Bobby go

And we fail to understand, Bobby
We fail to understand.

Francesca Beard has lived in London for many years and is not bored yet. She regularly performs at home and away as a poet and also with beautiful mutant Charley Marlowe, fusing folk to hop.
You can read her works in *Cheap: The Millionaire of New Ideas* or collect them in bite-sized chunks from the many 'zines and publications too fabulous to mention.

All of the Goodness, None of the Mess

Shrink wrapped conscience
and a dry-cleaned soul;
now you use a new religion–
rehabilitation.

Twelve steps and you hauled ass
up the ladder to clear skies,
caught the non stop express
to over the rainbow,
where your blue bird of liberty
chants in non-specific synergy.

O the group lifted your burden
and now you are light weight,
now you breach the bridge
between self and hate,
pontificating on your altered state
of emancipation.

All that tension's gone away
and the rope you walked on – tight usually –

the noose you spun from off your own neck
to lasso some herd-brained fool,
you've traded in
for a new leash of life.
You've grown bland with slack,
choosing contentment over friction,
lacking the substance you used to abuse.

I liked you better as a rabblerouser,
liked you more as mad carouser
at the gates of porn-shops,
nose pressed against the bars
of all London,
a wallower at waterholes,
happy as Lazarus, dead drunk but still rising.

I loved it when you turned the blow torch
of your mental processes
against innocent bystanders –
innocent of fucking what
– you said.
I loved it when you blew the short fuse,
amplified your views
from bar stools,
spewed your gut instincts out
on the back seats
of racist black cabs.
I loved you when you rose
like a shark
to the bait,
flayed the passing traffic
with the skin of your teeth,

cruising cursing down high streets
and the inebriant aisles
of the Tesco Metro.

I loved you when you screwed
anything that moved
just because you could.
I loved you when you felt so degraded the next day
that you said – what's the bollocks point anyway
– and did it again, that night
with some new same old same old.

I loved you because you fought
with your back to the wall of
indifference
and ignorance
and apathy.

I loved you because you took no prisoners
but threw them the keys
from the parapets,
before you turned and dived, heroic
into the next line

I loved you because you cried like a child
at injustice
and intolerance
and bad made for tv minidramas.

I loved you cause you thought that charity was ridiculous
but you'd buy a pint for a chiselling geezer that made you laugh,
even though it was your last fiver,

and only ten o'clock
and you yourself were an alcoholic.

I loved you for your lust for life
and truth and other people's wives.

At rehab, they cleaned you out.
Sardonic irrigation –
all your bitterness was washed away
in a warm spray.
Whitewashed your dark side and now you are whole.
Now you are unrecognisable.
They cauterized your wounds –
it deadened your nerve.
They sucked out the poison
and with it your passion.
Lobotomy comes to mind –
They healed you with a right old stitch up.

If I were a true friend I would be glad –
well, maybe – but the fire in your belly
has died,
having nothing to feed upon,
dampened by some perverse irony
that gave you life
but took it away.
It's good you love yourself.
I'm not going to.

The Poem That Was Really a List

the spade that was really a symbol
the queen that was really a son
the king that was really a rock star
the mad-man that was really God
the milk-man that was really dad
the waitress who was really an actress
the actress who was really an artist
the artist who was really a pornographer
the small boy who was really a helicopter
the vehicle that was really a toy
the toy that was really a bribe
the toy poodle that was really a baby
the baby that was really a last ditch attempt
the cafe latte that was really a milky coffee
the soup that was really a meal in itself
the studio flat that was really a bed-sit
the short-cut that was really a cul-de-sac
the nine-to-five that was really a ball and chain
the pain-free diet that was really a cash-loss weight gain
the commercial success that was really a sell-out failure
the cheque that was really in the mail
the lack of interest that was really impotence
the frigid cocktease that was really lack of interest
the one night stand that was really a date rape
the mercy fuck that was really an act of love
the leaked statement that was really a press release
the statistic that was really a cooked book
the apology that was really an excuse
the excuse that was really a screw you
the anecdote that was really an extended slap in the face

the helping hand that was really a kick in the teeth
the stiff upper lip that was really a cold shoulder
the last laugh that was really an own goal
the little bird that was really a can of worms
the fresh start that was really a wrong turn
the youthful radiance that was really soft focus
the race riot that was really a political protest
the spiritual journey that was really an ego trip
the ego trip that was really a spiritual journey
the home that was really an investment
the marital relations that were really a form of rent
the sofa that was really a bed
the park bench that was really a bed
the cynic who was really a romantic
the romantic who was really a sexist
the sexist who was really a phobic
the self-sufficiency that was really insecurity
the love that was really fear
the fear that was really nothing
the ending that was really nearly here.

Paul Birtill was born in Walton, Liverpool in 1960 and is half Irish. He moved to London in his early twenties and apart from a brief period in Glasgow has lived there ever since. As well as verse he writes plays, one of which was shortlisted for the Verity Bargate Award. Another play was performed at the Pentameters Theatre, Hampstead.

79 Kingfield

There wasn't much room
in our house so I crashed
in Ma's room 'til I was ten.

Sometimes she'd get up and
piss in an orange bucket
Quite often she'd see something
and call out
I hated the night . . .

Occasionally the old man
would creep in, tip-toe
past my bed and give
her one, unaware I was
awake listening.
They were both in their fifties
I hated the night . . .

She became ill and
moaned with pain
throughout the night
getting up to take

pills walk about
and piss in the orange bucket.
The old man stopped coming . . .

When I was ten my
dad built an attic on
the roof and I got my own room
small though it was
the nights were peaceful,
I learnt to sleep . . .

Waiting For My Mother

Fifty-three and totally grey
Wishing to avoid the
young mothers — was always
        last to arrive.
I could wait twenty minutes
and then, when the road was clear
in an old coat, looking tired
        and perhaps
        a little embarrassed
        She'd appear.
I was always pleased to
see her — well worth
waiting for was my old mum.

Dating

I always give a heil Hitler salute
on my first date and rant on about
badger baiting.
I never show my good side,
they always bugger off.

Sometimes I smack myself in the face,
refuse to buy a round, or talk about
life in a mental hospital.
I never show my good side,
they always bugger off.

But usually I just get steaming drunk
and talk of human scum — this one never
fails to alienate and send them on the run . . .

Born in Nottingham, **David Boulter** is the keyboard player in the Tindersticks and moved to London with the band in 1986. They have released eleven singles and six albums, including *The Second Tindersticks Album* from which 'My Sister' in taken. David Boulter is married and now lives in Prague.

My Sister

You remember my sister? How many mistakes did she make with those never blinking eyes? I couldn't work it out – I swear she could read mind, your life, the depths of your soul at one glance. Maybe she was stripping herself away, saying 'Here I am, this is me, I am yours and everything about me, everything you see, if only you look hard enough'. I never could.

Our life was a pillow fight, we'd stand there on the quilt, our hands clenched ready, her with her milky teeth, so late for her age, and a Stanley knife in her hand. She slashed the tyres on my bike and I couldn't forgive her.

She went blind at the age of five, we'd stand at the bedroom window and she'd get me to tell her what I saw. I described the houses opposite, the little patch of grass next to the path, the gate with its rotten hinges, forever wedged open that dad was always going to fix. She'd stand there quiet for a moment, I thought she was trying to develop the images in her own head, then she'd say –

'I can see little twinkly stars – like christmas tree lights in far away windows, rings of brightly coloured rocks revolving around orange and mustard planets. I can see huge tiger-striped fishes chasing tiny blue and yellow dashes – all tails and fins and bubbles.'

I'd look at the grey house opposite and close the curtains.

She burned down the house when she was ten, I was away camping with the Scouts, the fireman said she'd been smoking in bed, the old story I thought. The cat and our mum died in the flames so dad took us to stay with our aunt in the country. He went back to London to find us a new house, we never saw him again.

On her thirteenth birthday she fell down the well in our aunt's garden and broke her head, she'd been drinking heavily. On her recovery her sight had returned, a fluke of nature everyone said, that's when she said she'd never blink again. I would tell her when she stared at me, with her eyes wide and watering, that they reminded me of the well she fell in to, she liked this, it made her laugh.

She moved in with her gym teacher when she was fifteen, all muscles he was, he lost his job when it all came out and couldn't get another one, not in that kind of small town, everybody knew everyone else's business. My sister would hold her head high though – she said she was in love. They were together for five years until one day he lost his temper and hit her over the back of the neck with his Bullworker.

She lost the use of the right side of her body, he got three years but was out in fifteen months. We saw him a while later, coaching a non-league football team in a Cornwall seaside town. I don't think he recognised us, my sister had put on a lot of weight from being in the chair all the time. She'd get me to stick pins in and stub out cigarettes on her right hand, she'd laugh like mad because it didn't hurt. Her left hand was pretty good though, we'd have arm wrestling matches, I'd have to use both arms and she'd still beat me.

We buried her when she was thirty-two, me and my aunt, the vicar, and the man that dug the hole. She said she didn't want to be cremated and wanted a cheap coffin so the worms could get to her quicker, she said she liked the idea of it, though I thought it was because of what happened to the cat and our mum.

Eleanor Brown was born in 1969. As an English child growing up in Scotland, she learned early about racial feeling, being personally blamed for the beheading of Mary, Queen of Scots, and being ostracised during a primary school trip to the site of the Battle of Bannockburn. She claims that these formative experiences did not embitter her. After reading English Literature at York University, she became a menial in the banqueting department of a Cambridge hotel, and a Pizza Express waitress. She later travelled in France, where she lived for a while in a convent, and on returning to England took up her new post as barmaid in a North London pub. She lives in New Barnet in Hertfordshire.

IX

I don't know what you want from me. We talk
about a lot of things, but never that.
And if I asked, I'd break the tacit rules
of this as-modern-as-they-come affair –
this marvellous, no-strings, no-rules affair;
this minefield of exact, unwritten rules
surrounded by barbed wire of silence. That
is something of a pity, since we talk
about a lot of things, but I don't know –
and maybe never will, since if I asked
I'd break the tacit rules – quite what you want
from me – and minefields (modern ones) with no
strings (just barbed wire) we cross with care, unasked
questions buried, like so much else we want.

Joe Cairo, born on 29th February 1960, hails from Penge, and is a
lifelong resident of 'sarf' London. He has worked as an electrician,
warehouseman, bailiff and meter reader. Since 1968 he has been a Chelsea
fan, and since 1989 a hard-edged poet, chronicling the less salubrious
underside of urban life and running the performance poetry club that he co-
founded with Vic Lambrusco, the Hard Edge. He has met Prince Charles.

Drums and Flags

I was driven by the drums, inspired by the flags
and the people I once marched with call me slag,
it's so easy to condemn but I was only twenty-one
anti-semitic I thought you bought that in a chemist,
and a nigger-hating redneck that was never me.
So, don't be too quick to condemn.
I was only twenty one, that was then, dark days,
this is now.
Then I hated everyone,
the boss
the police,
college boys, everyone who had, which I had not.
An education don't make me laugh, they only taught
kids like me woodwork.
Second class, that's how I was made to feel.
A poxy job, work with your hands, but when I
balled them up and made a fist, I found another use.
The drums and the flags gave me a chance
to use my hands for something other than work.
HURT, PUNCH, KICK, STAB, SLASH, SMASH.

The beat of the drums made me pick up my feet.
The flying flags made me feel first class.
No longer in lower remove like at school,
when I marched with the front, I was no one's fool.
So don't be so quick to condemn, I was only twenty-one,
and politics was the last thought in my head . . .
I wanted them dead, every last one of them.
My fists would leave their mark on their superior faces.
A working class boy who was made to belong,
following the flags and drums.
But – slowly – I realised I was being used like a tool,
being used like a hammer, cannon fodder for ideals.
I never sought to understand.
And all the time fat leaders shouted their orders
from the back:
ATTACK, ATTACK, ATTACK!
Use your hands, that's all your good for.
And I thought, this has a familiar ring, the penny drops.
I stopped. And told them this is wrong, I'm working class,
and you're telling me to kick working class arse.
I QUIT, YOU'RE WRONG, I DON'T BELONG.
And the people I once marched with and called brother,
call me slag, black-lover, jew-lover,
those who were brothers turned their hate and
fists on me: Fascist. What's a Fascist?
And a nigger-hating redneck, that was never me.
I was only twenty-one and on the bottom of the rung.
But I looked up and saw the truth,
AND NOW I FEEL ASHAMED.

Chelsea vs Pablo Picasso

I've got a date, but Chelsea's at home, an never mind
It's at the Tate — Picasso you said
Did he play for Inter Milan?
No, he's an artist
OK, I'll come and stay a while, why not
after all it's only Chelsea's last home game of the season.

I steel myself with a good few pints; you turn up looking
    really nice.
First stop's the Poetry Library; she never told me this
I steal three books. My excuse I'm pissed
and outside it's raining. I wish I'd brought my mac.
It's nice and dry at Stamford Bridge.

Queuing at the Tate and I'm getting fucking soaked,
all my fags have gone soggy, can't even have a smoke,
and Chelsea's playing at The Bridge.
The things I do for love
or the promise of it.

Once inside the Tate we start the gallery shuffle,
shuffle, shuffle
shuffle, shuffle
the things I'll do these days to get a date with you
even miss watching the Blues.
Stop and look impressed, have a good long stare at Pablo's
    work
I don't fit in here, I'm feeling like a jerk,
but I shuffle round the Tate.

Figure no. 4 called 'Iron Wire and Cotton Reel',
worth fucking millions.
Is this shit for real?
Christ I'm bored, I wonder what the score is . . .
ART, there's no pretending, I don't like it
but I shuffle on.

Another room, bigger brighter, shuffle shuffle, be polite
but I'm trying hard to supress my laughter as I stop at
    exhibit no. 75
'Painted Steel Rods'.
A shuffler in front gasps in awe
and I don't think I can take anymore.

No. 116 is called 'The Cat'. Well it don't look like mine,
    and that's a fact.
No. 118 'The Goat' – this is bollocks,
and still it's raining outside and I ain't got a coat –
so I'll shuffle on round the Tate, at least it's dry in here
just like Stamford Bridge.

No. 148 is called 'Woman on the Beach'
I've seen no-one like that in Brighton,
152, 'Large Profile', eyes on the bleeding nose, ear on the
    head.
Now the walls are starting to close in on me
and I can only think of Chelsea.
Pablo's art has done my fucking head in.
My shuffle turns into a run,
got to get free of this place,
it's not my idea of fun.

So I sprint to the nearest pub
and it's packed with Pablo fans shuffling to the bar.
I wish I'd gone to Stamford Bridge
this is one art gallery too far.

I barge my way past the Art loving tossers
and order two pints
I sink them quickly. You come in asking
'Did you enjoy it?', 'No' I said 'It's shit'
You called me a 'savage git'
well that's it then date over
and I could have been watching Chelsea.

You shuffle out of the door
don't think I'll see you anymore
I go back to the bar
and ask the question
'anyone know the Chelsea score?'
and a voice from the shed said
'Chelsea four, Picasso nil'
Oh yes indeed — nuff said!

The Ugly

I want to get ugly, ugly with drink
I want to get so fucking ugly
that I can no longer think
no longer talk and become unable to walk
I wanna be the ugliest man in the bar
Ugliness is beautiful, ugliness is total

and I want to be the ugliest man in my local
So drink up and transform
from the swan to the ugly duckling
Drink so much that you can't help chuckling
at some poor bastard's misfortune
O.K, I know these days it costs a fortune
but look on it as an investment
I'll stand, or usually fall, by this statement
Being ugly with drink
brings out the real you
so, come to the bar, join me for a drink
or two, or three, or five
It's the one place where only the really ugly
can survive
Drinking so much that your brain
and your liver
are scarred from the inside –
It will make you stand out in a crowd
The truly ugly can't hide
and the beautiful people are scared
to look you head on in the bloodshot eyes
I wanna be so grotesque
I wanna be so disformed
I wanna be so blind drunk that I can't see
I wanna drown all the pleasant thoughts
inside me
because I don't like the world I see
when sober
So, come to the bar and have a drink or three
Come to the bar and get ugly, just like me
It's so fucking beautiful, just wait and see

Nick Cave is one of the most exciting and original songwriters currently working in rock music. His recordings with his band, The Bad Seeds, continue to attract wide praise and a huge international following, and he is also known for several memorable film appearances. His novel *And the Ass Saw the Angel* (Black Spring Press, 1989) was one of the most acclaimed literary debuts of recent years. *King Ink II* (Black Spring Press, 1997) is Nick's second collection of song lyrics and other writings.

Time Jesum Transeuntum Et Non Revertentum

We were called to the forest and we went down
A wind blew warm and eloquent
We were searching for the secrets of the universe
And we rounded up demons
And forced them to tell us what it all meant
We tied them to trees and broke them down one by one
On a scrap of paper they wrote these words
And as we read them the sun broke through the trees
'Dread the passage of Jesus for He will not return'
Then we headed back to our world and left the forest behind
Our hearts singing with all the knowledge of love
But somewhere, somehow we lost the message along the way
And when we got home we bought ourselves a house
And we bought a car that we did not use
And we bought a cage and two singing birds
And at night we'd sit and listen to the canaries' song
For we'd both run right out of words
Now the stars they are all angled wrong
And the sun and the moon refuse to burn
But I remember a message in a demon's hand
Dread the passage of Jesus for He does not return

Nobody's Baby Now

I've searched the holy books
Tried to unravel the mystery of Jesus Christ the Saviour
I've read the poets and the analysts
Searched through the books on human behaviour
I travelled the whole world around
For an answer that refused to be found
I don't know why and I don't know how
But she's nobody's baby now

I loved her then and I guess I love her still
Hers is the face I see when a certain mood moves in
She lives in my blood and skin
Her wild feral stare, her dark hair
Her winter lips as cold as stone
Yeah, I was her man
But there are some things even love won't allow
I held her hand but I don't hold it now
I don't know why and I don't know how
But she's nobody's baby now

This is her dress that I loved best
With the blue quilted violets across the breast
And these are my many letters
Torn to pieces by her long-fingered hand
I was her cruel-hearted man
And though I've tried to lay her ghost down
She's moving through me, even now
I don't know why and I don't know how
But she's nobody's baby now

Actor and comedian **Craig Charles**, best known as Lister from the *Red Dwarf* series, revealed yet another talent with his first collection of poetry called *No Other Blue* (Penguin, 1998). Craig has been writing poems for some years and many of them have featured on television's *Saturday Night Live* and *Wogan*, and radio's *Loose Ends*. They cover a range of subjects, from personal (prison poems and poems about his mother's final illness) to the political (old people dying of hypothermia, South Africa's official recognition of interracial sex). His poems combine outrageous humour with a sense of the poignant, and the lyrical with the narrative.

Family Way

My mother sits alone and knits
Bonny boots for auntie's newborn baby
Father sits alone and spits
Right into the grate,
And tells my mum
To shift her bum
The dinner's getting late

And our Jimmy's coming home in spring
– Did eighteen months for robbing things
Like houses, cars and wedding rings,
And all those things
That are in between.

And our Julie's in the club again,
And when asked I'm sure she'll say
She has no luck with men.

And when I'm asked
I'm sure I'll say
That I've been in
The family way.

My dad took me aside and said:
'Don't dare go down the pier head —
The ships have gone, the water's black,
With dirty men, with long black macs
Weaving dirty drunken tracks,
And leaving dirty drunken paths.'

But I guess my dad just can't relax
Since he got sacked.

For thirty years he broke his back
Till work got slack.
And now he goes
And drinks his dole
In public houses
Battered by the times.

And mum wakes up and cries at home
And grandma calls her on the phone,
And when she's asked, I'm sure she'll say
That she's been in the family way.
And when we're asked, I'm sure we'll say
We've all been in the family way.

Our Julie's only seventeen
She works in some launderette.
She doesn't like it very much —
It's all that she could get.

She's getting married pretty soon,
All dressed in virgin white.
Mother said that's what she'd like —
She wants her kids to do it right.

So our Jimmy stole
A wedding ring,
So she could have
The real thing.
And he got caught
And that's what
Bad luck brings.

And when he's asked,
I'm sure he'll say
That he's been in
The family way.

Billy Childish is a legendary figure in underground writing, painting and music and has appeared on over eighty independent albums. He was formerly in The Pop Rivets, The Milkshakes and Thee Mighty Caesars, and his present band is Thee Headcoats. He has been called one of Britain's genuine, if genuinely unsung heroes. 'The Bitter Cup' first appeared on the LP *At The Bridge* and was performed by Billy with The Singing Loins, and 'You Make Me Die' appeared on the album *Acropolis Now* and was performed by Thee Mighty Caesars. He paints and writes in Chatham.

The Bitter Cup

and i remember the breath of my father
his kisses were bearded and damp
the romance of the bottle dragging him down
to awaken dishevelled in the tank

and theres no sea deeper than the piss of the bottle
and none speaks the truth like the drunk
whisky runs thru me like a sorrowful river
im down on my knees and im sunk

and i remember my mother hitting the gin
she fell and we thought she was dead
naked and doll-like
his skull face was shouting
we ran to our room painted red

hot for women we curse and abuse them
they say we aint got no respect
full of bravado godless and fearful
we pray no one will detect

and theres no taste sweeter than the rush of hot vomit
sieved thru decaying back teeth
id whisper i love you
and quit all this hating
but in truth i aint got the belief

smashed and dishevelled
of course they did wreck us
poisoned by our own bitter cup
stumbling and hoping inside i was lonely
im sick and im down and
im drunk

You Make Me Die

well there's a feeling in this world
that causes unrest
your ambition and success
is what i detest
I try to be true
I'm trying my best
I'm not seduced by your cheap love
hatreds and mess
you make me die

I heard all you gotta say
I heard it in school
about your soft soap sex
and your sickly drool
but you only care for yourself

you're just like all the rest
you love your filthy god
and think you're the best
you make me die

TVs videos money and vice
will get you crawling on the floor
like a sucking lice
you'll swallow seed
before you'll take advice
well someone should of told you girl
that ain't very nice
you make me die

John Citizen has performed on the BBC, Channel 4, MTV and ABC, and has featured frequently on national and local radio. His work has been published in magazines such as *Avaganda*, *Postcard*, *Poetry Quarterly*, *All Mouth*, *Affectiona 11*, *Punch* and anthologies such as *The Fire People* and the *London Cafe Book*. He regularly reviews poetry and has worked in mixed media with Poetry on Buses and Poetry on Walls.

Live, he has appeared at many festivals including Edinburgh, Glastonbury, Cheltenham, the London International Festival of Literature, Austin International Poetry Festival and all other usual and unusual venues.

He is the resident MC at the Poetry Café in Covent Garden, London.

The Library of Love

I WAS OUT OF DATE AND ANTIQUARIAN,
YOU DUSTED ME OFF, YOU'RE THE LIBRARIAN.
MY PAGES WERE LOOSE, I WAS UNWINDING.
YOU STAPLED ME TOGETHER, YOU'RE MY BINDING.
FRIGHTENED TO WEAR MY HEART
ON MY SLEEVE BLURB,
TOO MANY NOUNS, YOU WERE THE VERB.
THE END OF MY LINES WERE WELL OVERDUE,
YOU PAID ALL MY FINES, YOU CAN RENEW.
I WANTED TO BE A LOAN,
YOU TOOK ME OUT.
I WAS AT A LOSS LEADER,
YOU'RE MY PROOF READER.
WHEN NO ONE CREDITED ME, YOU EDITED ME.
AND WHEN CRITICS RUBBISHED ME,
YOU PUBLISHED ME.
FROM THE SHELVES BELOW TO THE SHELVES ABOVE.
YOU'RE THE LIBRARIAN IN THE LIBRARY OF LOVE.

Brendan Cleary lives in exile from Co. Antrim in Newcastle, where he edited and survived *The Echo Room*. He works as a part-time lecturer, performance poet and stand-up comic. His last book-length collection, *Sacrilege*, was published by Bloodaxe in 1998.

Helen's Boyfriend

& I think nice jacket captain, nice cloth,
pity about the utter fuckwit inside though
& he obviously has impressed her, obviously,
what with all that flicking about of her hair,
all that pretending not to understand, wide-eyed
& if she marries this eejit I'll disintegrate,
already in the middle of the night I sweat
& I go to the bog & feel I'm composed of dots,
no matter to speak of, I'm just dots darting
all over the shop & look at his tie, christ,
is he wearing that for a bet & she looks at me
& I look back longingly like a cocker spaniel
& she looks at him, his greasy bake & he leers
so I get up real polite, make tame excuses
with my head still intact, I phrased it later . . .

Last Orders

My ex-wife with her cuddly dog
is with her lover's ex-mistress
who is talking seductively
to my brother's ex-girlfriend
& her partner now a lesbian too
who once had designs on me
before my boss's sister
left a message on my answerphone
saying my best mate's girl
really fancies me at least sometimes

It's all getting mighty confusing,
I thought
& I only popped in for a swift one
on the way over to my mum's . . .

Art

Tossing her blond curls about so haphazardly too,
tearing into the bites & nibbles as I approached.
This Derek, he's a conceptual artist, prizewinner.
Do you eat fresh sardines, then save the bones for him.
Derek's building a city for the Millennium this week,
he needs bones for roof slates, he'll paint them blue.
Art in all its many guises is no bother to this lad,
he once dressed up as Trotsky & went on the dodgems,
he once punctured the heart of a sheep with an ice-pick,
every third Tuesday he doesn't sleep or eat, a protest.

Her mouth agape & blubbering she fled into the kitchen
pleading *Gloria, get me out of this madhouse*, squealing,
they're all mad, flipping mad as spoons, Gloria, help!
But Gloria had slipped upstairs into Derek's studio,
poking about, utterly transfixed by the cow on wheels,
the pigeons smeared in molasses, the mechanical insects.
& Gloria looked more than just a little bit excited too,
by the time the pair of them scarpered, slamming doors.
Around then Derek & I were leaning back on the cushions,
raising our champagne aloft, both in fits of giggles . . .

Jarvis Cocker was born thirty-five years ago in the post-industrial hamlet of Sheffield, the result of stolen moments at a Boxing Day party in High Green. A sickly child, he contracted meningitis at the age of five which left him with severely impaired vision. He has gone on to make this a fashion feature rather than a handicap which has resulted in writings such as the one featured in this publication.

N.B. Kelvin Flats were a large-scale high-rise development just outside Sheffield city centre – they have now been demolished to make way for a ciabatta factory.

Deep Fried In Kelvin

Oh children of the future: conceived in the toilets of Meadowhall to be raised on cheap corn snacks & garage food. Rolling empty cans down the stairwell – don't you love the sound? Like the thoughts of a bad social worker rattling round his head; trying to remember what he learned in training college. 'Mester said you wasn't allowed in here so why don't you get lost?' And if you're good when you grow up maybe you can live on Kelvin. Yeah, you can live in Kelvin & promenade the concrete walkways where pigeons go to die.

A woman on the 14th floor noticed that her ceiling was bulging as if under a great weight. When the council investigated they discovered that the man in the flat above had transported a large quantity of soil into his living room in which several plants he had stolen from a local park were growing. When questioned, the man said that all he wanted was a garden.

Oh God, I think the future has been deep fried. Deep Fried in Kelvin & now it's rotting behind the remains of a stolen motorbike. 'I never touched it, honest, but there was nothing else to do.' We don't need your sad attempts at social conscience based on taxi rides home at night from exhibition openings. We just want your car radio & bass reflex speakers. Now.

Suffer little children to come unto me & I will tend their adventure playground splinters & cigarette burns & feed them fizzy orange & chips, that they may grow up straight & tall: that they may grow up to live on Kelvin. Oh yeah, we can have ghettos too, only we use air rifles instead of machine guns. Stitch that. And we drink Diamond White.

In the end, the question you have to ask yourself is — 'Are you talking to me, or are you chewing a brick?' (Either way, you lose your teeth.)

Born and raised in Essex, poet and performer **Andrew Copeman** contributes regularly to the *Idler* magazine, in between restructuring his life. He has a naughty alter-ego in the form of Clive D'Arcy, and plans to reject vice for the millennium.

He is a snappy dresser, an occasional walker, a stalwart of the London scene, and does not suffer fools gladly.

Have You Met Clive D'Arcy (?)

The morning is monochrome through the blinds,
A photo-booth impression
For useless passports
All borders closed.

Crawling from twisted hung-over wreckage,
My delightful Prince of Wales check suit vomit encrusted,
I head for the drinks cabinet.
Harvey saves me.
Bristol creamed I slip into sharp black lines tailored to my mood
Paint it baby.

Outside's a grey blur.
Trees twist in 'can't be arsed mate' defeat and the
    pavement's one long travelator,
Ferrying me to the Terminal Departure lounge,
My local:
The Throat and Cancer.

Inside the place where everyone knows your pain,
I take a table by the door.
Dead shapes drift
And I tug my cuff-links.

The CD jukebox programmes the atmosphere,
Whitney Houston
The signal that we're lost.
Everyone looks like a road-traffic accident
Waiting for local press-coverage.

I catch reflections of myself,
In the sides of stale pints,
Floating fag-ends in the dregs
Aquatic ash-trays.

Cold in the stripped light,
Old inside this soft liqueured womb,
Dead to the touch
A washed-out unanswered question

Have you met me?

I am Clive D'Arcy,
Dashing young blade about town . . .

I Wouldn't Shoot You

At the Doctor's I sat with quiet dread
As he read the results of the tests.
'Is that good or bad?' I asked.
He leant over a photo of his mistress,
Lowered his specs
And replied;
'Well, you're not a thoroughbred,
But I wouldn't shoot you.'

Stuart David is 29, and married to wee Karn. He speaks and sings in Looper, and plays bass in Belle and Sebastian. His novel *Nalda Said* has just been published by IMP fiction.

Piano, Window, Piano

In the middle of summer, when it's raining outside and you're having a bit of a sofa day, it's sometimes good to imagine yourself as a minor character from history. Someone whose life you know very little about. Maybe even nothing.

Today I pretended to be a man who wrote a song for Elvis Presley. I'd watched Elvis Presley singing the song in a video — wearing expensive sunglasses and surrounded by an orchestra, gripping the microphone in a hand weighed down by precious stones and gold and a watch as big as a carriage clock.

And the song was supposed to be from him to Priscilla, after they had separated, to say how sorry he was, and how he was hurting.

So I gradually set about inventing the person whose feelings this song was really about, living it all the while as if it was me.

I began to see myself in the rain, somewhere in the early

part of the nineteen-seventies, walking along an American street at night with my heart in my shoes. And as I came slowly into focus I saw that I was wearing a long wool coat, with my hands buried deep in the pockets, and a worn out pair of Italian shoes.

I was on my way home from my office with the piano inside, but I didn't feel much like going home yet. Instead, I was going to stop off in a quiet little café I hadn't been to for a while – and have some dinner and a drink, until it was almost time to sleep. And who could tell; I might even buy a cigar there, and smoke it after I had eaten.

I'd spent most of the day at my office, walking from the piano to the window and back to my piano, writing most of the song Elvis Presley was going to sing. But there were still some gaps in the words, and I could work on them while I was eating and while I was having a drink afterwards, since the tune was fixed solid in my head.

Of course, I didn't know yet that Elvis Presley was going to sing the song. If I had done it might have made me feel a bit better. But I didn't, how could I? I couldn't even tell if it was a good song yet or not. It was just the only thing I'd been able to write, feeling the way I did – and it had felt good to be doing *anything* at this point in time.

This was my story, you see:

My office was up on the fifth floor, and whenever I looked out my window I could easily see into the offices on the fifth floor of the building opposite mine. There weren't any pianos in there; no one wrote songs in those offices. It was an insurance place. But there was this one woman who'd once worked in there, and the very first song I'd written in my office had been for her.

I'd written it in exactly the same way as I'd written today's song too. Piano, window, piano. But instead of being filled with a terrible ache each time I'd looked out, and instead of seeing nothing but the empty aisles where she used to walk, I'd seen the real woman herself while I'd been working on that one. And my heart had leapt every time I'd dared to gaze out.

That had been a very easy song. If the truth be known I hadn't even noticed I was writing it until it was finished. It was just something I'd been doing to try and prolong the gaps between my trips to the window – and something I'd done each time I leapt back from there, whenever I'd thought she was just about to catch me gawping at her.

It had turned out to be a good song though. And it had turned out to be a big hit too – when another famous singer had taken it up. And perhaps you won't believe this, but one night – soon after it had been released – I'd stepped out onto the pavement, and that woman had walked past me out there; and she was humming that tune to herself.

I couldn't believe it, and for a moment I didn't know what to do. I was caught between wanting to talk to her about it, and being too nervous to speak. But, in the end, I just had to stop her.

'Excuse me,' I said, as she stared warily at me. 'This may seem a bit strange, but . . . I wonder if you could tell me the name of that song you were singing.'

'Of course.' she said, looking somewhat relieved. And she uttered the words I'd written at the top of the page, the first day I'd seen her.

And then, just before she started walking again, she said: 'It's my favorite song just now.'

I thought − for a while − that I was going to end up arrested out there, as I tried first of all to convince her that I'd written the song, and then that I'd written it for her. I could tell she thought I was crazy, but I couldn't give up. And I explained all about our offices − and how she would see me up there if she looked out of her window the next day.

And the following afternoon, after we had waved to each other across the gap above the streets, I'd convinced her to meet me for lunch. And the following year, after we'd driven out to the beach one day, I'd convinced her to marry me too. But that was a long time ago now. A long way back in the past.

I'd written a whole bunch of hit songs for her after that first one; a whole bunch of happy songs. But I suppose, for too long, I'd done too much of that. Spent too much time on it, rather than with her. And now, here I was in the rain, with most of the words for my sad song buried deep in my wool-coat pocket.

And then I heard a noise. A clunk and a whirr. And I was staring at the TV screen again. Sitting on my orange sofa back in 1997, as the video began to rewind itself. And I pressed 'Play' to have one more look at that enormous wristwatch on the screen. It really was quite fantastic. A rectangle the full width of Elvis Presley's wrist and twice as long, with a face surrounded by diamonds.

And as I closed my eyes and listened closely to the words of the song he was singing, I decided I had done a good job on filling in the gaps at the café.

But I did feel a bit guilty for having smoked the cigar.

Jegsy Dodd is not a 60s arty poet who would read verse to intellectual snobs but a lad who could interest the masses in poetry, surely the most difficult task in showbiz apart from being Jimmy Tarbuck's minder in a walkabout round Liverpool.

Giro Day

The latch from the gate awoke me
I suddenly became alive
I saw the vision from the bedroom window
The cheque had finally arrived
I spontaneously human combusted with lust
Followed by a Mexican wave
I did The Shake 'n Vac and put the freshness back
And did the dance of the Seven Veils
I cartwheeled down the steepest stairs
In a state of full undress
Then grabbed the postman by his sack
And screamed 'Yes!' 'Yes!' 'Yes!'

Because hey-hey-hey, it's Giro Day
I'm so happy I could cry
Hey-hey-hey it's Giro Day
And I'm H.A.P.P.Y.

Kissed the Landlord on the lips
Made love to the next door neighbour
Got a stabbing pain between my hips
I thought I'd gone into labour
Broke wind with all the excitement

Broke sweat as the Post Office beckoned
Broke Roger Bannister's record
By a minute and twenty seconds
Sang *Nessun Dorma* to the Post Office clerk
As I tried to give her the eye
Produced my I.D. – a photo of me
On holiday when I was five

So with my beer vouchers in my pocket
I gave the Post Office door a boot
Did a forwards roll to the edge of the kerb
And gave a clenched fist salute
I screamed hey-hey-hey it's Giro Day
I'm so happy I could die
Hey-hey-hey it's Giro Day and I'm H.A.P.P.Y.

So through a drunken haze to the end of the day
From the bookies to the pub
To the takeaway
Past the fairweather friends
Whose acquaintance I had made
Who enjoyed all the drinks
While muggins here paid
Over cracks in the pavement
In the driving rain
To the house up on the hill
Where a lonely man stays
Ignoring the landlord who stood blocking my way
Obviously impressed by my kiss from earlier that day
To the room up the stairs
Where my body shall lay
Until the next time – the best time
Until Giro Day.

David Duff trained as a journalist. He has worked on many multi-media events, and runs poetry events in Glasgow and Bristol. In addition to written work he also presents his poetry in performance and on film.

The Blackest Man in the Universe

I, am the **Blackest** man in the universe,
  I may not look it but I am.

  I come   from four

  corners of   the world,

          Told to go BACK HOME . . .!
to Africa,
      Pakistan,
          the jungle
              and M-i-s-s-i-s-s-i-p-p-i . . .

I'm so fucking BLACK,
              ''Boots''
          doesn't have anything,
          in their range of natural products,
                  for my
              nubian skin.

In fact so colourful am I,
Drivers
      slow
          down to catch my eye,
              ¿Mums clutch handbags as I walk by?

The weather's much warmer where I was born . . .
Och aye.

So gather round me homeys, 'n' let me tell my stories,
Of days in da 'hood, where're ain't no good,
In the streets of . . . *Hillhead*,
tucked up . . . *in my bed*.

I, am <u>the</u> **Blackest**
        man in the

universe.
I may not look it, but I am.

The Edinbury Whoors perform as a group, and can be found at many mixed media events and happenings.
Sandie Craigie: Conscientious reprobate and Elvis cultist. Performed with Blocko Vomit and Koombayah.
'She's a rebel and she'll never be any good' (Jailbait Journal 1979).
Raoul Kawalsky: Sexually transmitted writer and anti-personnel performer. Hobbies include desecrating Nazi cemeteries. Makes a horrible sucking noise.
Ray Myles: The screaming schemie. What you get when Richard and Judy meet Mexican masked wrestling. Too many personalities, too little time.

A Want Ti Be
By **Sandie Craigie**

A want ti be
Blue lipped an rowdy haired
Loud, crass and ooty
Sinc
An accidental overdose
The chaos in a chaotic crowd
A car crash in yer neghbourhood
A shite friend an a great fuck
Bite through flesh an taste the blood
A wreck ae death an a smile ae thunder
The look ae love when there's nae face left
Hert strings stung wi a razor edge
Yer mother's crimes an
Yer ancient screams
An
Yer ancient screams
Am a fuckin bomb

Am the unexploded dream in yer last blank wank
Ave a nicegirl script that a never signed
An a dinny intend ti stick it oot

A've a short
Fuse
An a violent
Mind
Ti dispose
Ess
Yer under
Soul
Yer under
Class
Yer shattering
Smile
Am brekin
Up
A want
Control
A want
You
An a canny
Wait
Ti light the
Fuse an
Det
O
Nate

Politiks Ae Kissin
By **Sandie Craigie**

Sumtimes
Tired ae fightin wi
Peace an peace
A wid like tae take the
Distruction ae your embrace
An demolish mi
Lay doon an become
Whoor ti ye
Gie in ti the barbed wire ae
Teeth an words
Pit mooth tae mooth
An in a deep
Politikal kiss
Pull on the pin
On the hand grenade that
Is yer tongue an
Blaw ye ti fuck

Sumtimes
Am a pacifist

Enterprise

By **Sandie Craigie**

A want ti buy a Fayzer

A want ti be able ti say 'Captain's Log Stardate'

Withoot huvin ti think what folk'll think ae me a want ti
  meet Spock

A want ti go back, oan an oan ti the seventies

a want ti boldly go a want ti fuck Kirk

in fact, a want ti fuck Uhura come oan Scotty ya cunt ye
  beam me up!

am seek ae lightbulbs, pricks an kitchen politiks,

seek ae yer cuntin lies an catpish excuses

am seek ti fuck!

A want ti buy a silver pinny

a want ti find oot aboot Enterprise Allowance a want a
  joab!

cleanin the starship enterprise am cleanin the starship
  enterprise am seek,

am seek ae 'A can't communicate with you' Fuck Off!

A want ti go where it's aw there in the raise ae an
  eyebrow

a want ti speak Klingon

a want they light-years gie me they light-years

a want ti Star Trek

a want ti Trek Stars

a want ti buy   a fuckin   Fayzer

Cuttin' Legs
By **Raoul Kawalsky**

A was watching this one through the windy
There she was, calm as day, hacking all the legs oaf
Every single pair of ur man's breeks, oaf wi one leg
so A bangs on the windy
Huy what you up ti?
She gies me this silly wee face
like ur best pal'd just been hit by lighting or supm
and she beckons ees in

Nae cup ae tea or fuck all, by the way
she just takes ees inti the sitting room
shifts all the legs off the settee
and points that A've to sit doon
What's the Hamden? A say
It's ma Dougie she sais
Ees gonny have ees leg oaf
A sais what? and she cairries on
Ees ti huv it oaf by the next full moon
Where d'ye hear this? A sais
She tells ees. A goat a message she sais
A message? A sais, intrigued by now. Whae fi?
'That Posh Spice' she sais. 'She came ti ees in a dream
and said Dougie's ti huv ees leg oaf by the next full moon
A wisny convinced. An you believed ur?
Why no? she sais. Awfy talanted lassie.
A just wet away an left ur ti it, still nae sign ae a cup ae tea

Burial
By **Raoul Kawalsky**

A follied um
you ever thought how difficult that is
folly-in someone A mean
A follied um
aw the way up to the park
E went inti the bushes
E came oot again with this wee yelly spade
E dug a wee hole, A seen um.
takes the fish outty ees jacket
unwraps it
drops it in the hole
Scuffs the earth back in on top ae it
pats it doon wi the spade
Now, Am thinking, what the fuck?
E comes back doon the path and A stops um
Hey, A've been watching you
What d'you think you're on?
That wis a nice bit ae cod you hud there an it's nae use now
And e just smiles up at ees
Did A tell you e was really wee, this guy?
Anyway what e says is this:
The sky gods are displeased wi mankind
apparently
and it's fallen ti him ti appease thum
that's what e said, appease thum.
What's that then? A asks um
Oh A lay oot gifts for thum
an then maybe they won't destroy wur world
and aw God's creatures on it

Fuckin oddball
Seen um again on the Tuesday, but
Wet for a pint wi um
Shame ti see an old guy like that
by umsel
Goan aw funny and that

Handgun

By **Raoul Kawalsky**

Came back in,
she was still sittin there like a hangover.
Sais, Eh, you no moved, then?
She sais nuhin
A turns on the telly, she turns it ower ti the news
This guy's got off in the high court
Killed ees wife
bit the court accepted the hing wis pre-menstrual at the time
an puttin an awfy strain on thur marriage
So, they let um off
Bit radge, that? A sais ti ur
mair ti strike up conversation than anythin else
She sais fuck all
just starin at the telly an the guy's face
that fuckin gun in ur lap
loadin an unloadin the hing
ower an ower

I Wiz Nearly A Daddy Once
By **Ray Myles**

They said 8 weeks wisney long enough for it to
Be a boy or a girl
But I don't like the word 'IT'

I know it was her body her decision
And that she was torn up inside in ways
That I cannie come close to imagining

And aye ok ah do feel a bit shite
A bit rejected about her no wanting
A kid that was part of me

But it's no about that
It's none oh that macho bullshit
Sowing ma seed — none oh that fucked up illusions
Of immortality
Nah the thing I cant get ma heid round is see that
Gadgie over there F'n and C'ing at his bairn

She is just a wee toddler something has frightened her
Pick her up for Gods sake
Give her a cuddle — kiss away her tears

Ah cannie look anymair — That's what I cannie come to
    terms with
Tosspots and cold Bastards like him
Can have wains be a daddy

I wiz Nearly a Daddy Once.

Andrew Edwards a.k.a. Andy Sticks was born in London in 1966 – and is a firehorse (in astrological terms).

His poems are a reflection of his life/streetlife today. He likes to call his verse virtual anecdotes.

He has been performing on the stage and writing seriously for this past year, although he has been writing since he was eighteen.

Safer Steps

SNAPPY, WEARY AND SLIGHTLY TEARY
'ARE YOU OK?'
YOUR NIGHT TIME FRIENDS THEY TEND TO QUERY

A SCORE'S WHAT SHE NEEDS
HAVE YOU GOT IT TO LEND HER?
THOSE IMMORTAL WORDS RANG TRUE
THAT LAST BANK HOLIDAY WEEKENDER

DOLLED UP TO THE NINES
OUTFIT PLANNED WELL IN ADVANCE
ANOTHER 2 LINES
AND HEY . . .
HE'S THE GREATEST DANCER THAT I'VE EVER SEEN
IT'S THE LAST FRIDAY NIGHT FOR THAT BANK
    HOLIDAY QUEEN

COMPTONS, THE EDGE, BARCODE, SUB SOHO
HERE WE GO, HERE WE GO, HERE WE GO
UNTIL WE GO TO THE BAR AND THE ANSWER'S
    NO

STILL ITCHING TO GO
BUT I'M NOT TALKING RASH
WE HEAD FOR THE POINT THAT DISPENSES THE CASH
£150 SHOULD DO US
LET'S GO AND GIVE IT SOME OF THAT

FRIDAY NIGHT WITH THE BIG FULL MOON
JUST TURNED INTO SATURDAY AFTERNOON
DJ PLAY ME
ONE MORE TUNE, ONE MORE TUNE, ONE MORE TUNE

'FROM WHAT I HEAR THEY'RE UP FOR A LOCK-IN'
REPORTED A MAN IN FISHNET STOCKINGS
'LATER, TO THAT MATE!
ANYONE GOT THE TIME?'
THE NEXT THING I KNOW IT'S ALL BACK TO MINE

SUP-UP, SPLIF-UP, KNEES-UP, NOSE-UP,
TWO QUEENS ON THE SOFA
ONE A BIT LIGHT ON HER LOAFERS
THEY OFFER TO PICK SOME MORE UP . . .

I LOUNGE ON MY PARKER KNOLL
AS THEY RISE FROM THEIR SEAT
SNAKE SKIN LOAFERS ENVELOP ONE PAIR OF FEET

FROM THE SYSTEM PUMPING RHYTHMS
A TAPE COURTESY OF CARL COX
ON HER PLATES SHE WEARS SHOES
KNOCK OFF PATRICK COX
YOU CAN BET YOUR LIFE SHE GETS HER ROOTS
    TOUCHED UP
AT A SHOP CALLED ROX

AND ANOTHER THING THE POX
SEE HER, SHE LOOKS THE TYPE
WHO WILL ONE DAY HAVE A DOSE
GROSS

ANYWAY, THE TWO OFF TO RE-STOCK
BUT NOT THE NEW AGE HIPPY
THE THING IN THE FOOTWEAR
IT STARTS TO GET LIPPY
UNAWARE THAT NEW LEATHER SOLES
ON SHAGPILE CAN BE DANGEROUSLY SLIPPY

I SUDDENLY GET VERTICAL
TO NIP THIS IN THE BUD
AND OVER HE GOES IN HIS LOAFERS
AND HITS THE DECK WITH A THUD

HE NEVER CAME ROUND

THE CORONER'S REPORT
IT WAS RATHER GORY
BUT AS HE SAID THERE'S A MORAL TO THIS STORY

'ALWAYS GIVE YOUR NEW LEATHER SOLES A BIT
   OF A RUB DOWN
WITH SANDPAPER BEFORE VENTURING OUT FOR A
   NIGHT ON THE TOWN!'

Lucy English was born in Sri Lanka. She grew up in London and studied English and American Literature at the University of East Anglia. She has an M A in creative writing from Bath Spa University.

In March 1996 Lucy won the Bristol Poetry Slam and has been performing poetry ever since. She has toured Holland and Denmark and has performed at Festivals all over the U K. Her first novel, *Selfish People* was published by Fourth Estate in 1998 and her second novel, *Children of Light* was published in 1999.

Lucy lives in Bristol and has three children. She is currently working on a third book.

Let Me Be

Let me be. Let me be. Let me be . . .
Your slut.
You know the one you ring up when you've had a row
    with your girlfriend.
And there she is. In a top that's too tight and a skirt that's
    too short.
And you can have her.
You can have her in the hall, and on the stairs and in the
    bathroom and on the bog.
You can have her anywhere.

Let me be. Let me be. Let me be . . .
Your drunk slut.
You know the one that's been hanging around the bar all
    evening
With that hungry look on her face.
And now it's closing time

And you're the last decent cock that still works.
And here she comes.
A bit old and faded. A bit unsteady.
But you don't care because you've had eight pints of
    Otterhead to cloud your judgement
And besides, you're up for it.
So you invite her home, but you don't actually get there.
You land up in an alleyway that smells of cider and cat's
    piss and elderflowers.
And there you are shagging her against a fence
In a tangle of pulled down pants and trousers.
And when you do get home you fall asleep straight away in
    a chair
And you don't hear her flitting about your house
Like a trapped bird.

Let me be. Let me be. Let me be . . .
Your mad drunk slut.
You know the one who rings you up twenty times a day
    even when you're at work.
You know the one who sends you six love letters a week,
Then runs screaming after you because she saw you go into
    a shop with another woman.
You know the one who's always hiding behind that bush in
    your front garden
So when you leave your house you're never quite sure
    whether she's there or not.
You know the one who's always peering in through your
    windows
And where did you leave your binoculars?
You know the one who's so good at disguises you're never
    quite sure

Whether she's that old lady walking her dog
Or she's that man with a beard on the bus.
You know the one who stands outside your door for an
    hour in the rain
Until you let her in.
Until you let her in.
Just so that you can talk to her.
Just so that you can say to her, 'Please. Leave. Me. Alone.'
But somehow it never gets to that.
Somehow it's always the same.
It's you on the sofa with your pants down and one thought
    going through your head.
Oh, no.
Oh, no.
Oh yes . . .

Let me be. Let me be. Let me be . . .
You evil, mad, drunk slut.
Because she's so mad she knows exactly what she's doing.
She's getting through to you.
She's getting through to you.
She's becoming you.
She is you.

And you cannot extinguish her.
You cannot extinguish her no matter how hard you thrust.
Like the moth that flies into the candle again and again.
Ftt. Ftt. Ftt.
Fizzling with desire as you burn in the flame
Of your crafty, evil, mad, drunk slut.

Your angel.

Liar

I'm a liar. I'm a fake.
My hair's dyed. It's a wig.
I'm 52 years old.
I'm made of silicone.

This leg is rubber, you'd never guess.
I'm bionic. I'll live to be 200
but my brain is as sharp as steel.
I take smart drugs every ten minutes.
I can do the Independent crossword.
I can translate ancient Greek to Egyptian and back again.
I can speak Croatian.

I'm a liar. I'm a phoney.
I'm not trendy. I'm tricking you.
I don't wear these clothes at home.
I wear fluffy pink slippers and a blue nylon housecoat
and curlers in the bath.
I have gold taps and deep pile shag maroon carpets.

I like Sky TV. I like Oasis.
I like Val Doonican and James Last and military bands and
    Highland pipers.
I wear a kilt. I'm really Scottish, och aye. I'm really Irish.
    I'm really Belgian.
I'm really Japanese. I'm really a Christian. I'm really the
    virgin Mary.
I'm really a virgin.
I hate sex. It's messy and sticky. I hate men.

No I don't. I am a man and I'm British and I love my
    country.
I raise the flag on Sundays. I like shooting pheasants. I
    don't believe in poverty.
I'm in the army. I'm in the SAS. I was in the Falklands. I
    was in the Gulf war.
I was in the Gurkhas. The regiment. The Queen. God bless
    her.

I am the Queen. I'm the Queen's twin sister surgically
    altered
and hidden away for years with a peasant family in a
    bungalow in Woking,
and I have now come to claim my title and start a war.

No I haven't. I'm a liar. I'm an alien and I have come
    from another galaxy
and a loop in the time-space continuum.
Because we are the guardians of the universe
and we have been watching you for centuries,
and you have disappointed us.

No you haven't. I love you. I love you all. I love all of
    you.
We are full of love.
Feel the love. Can't you feel it, flowing like a river
    between us.

I'm a liar. I don't love you.
It wasn't an orgasm. I was looking at the ceiling and I saw
    a spider and I shouted out 'It's huge!'
I don't love you.

I love my window cleaner.
I love that man down there
and I want his babies and I want to get married and live in
    a truck
and be happy and free and uncomplicated
And his dick is bigger than yours.
Let's be friends. You will always be my friend.

I'm a liar. I didn't write this.
Simon Armitage wrote this because he writes everything.
I'm a liar. I didn't write this my eight-year-old son wrote this
because he's a genius and I keep him locked in his bedroom
and I make masses of money out of his poems.
Masses and masses of money.
No I don't.
I'm a liar.
I wrote this. This is the truth.

Make Me A Modern Christian Song

Make me a modern Christian song,
and one that you can sing along to
with a tune that isn't too complicated
and words that hardly ever rhyme.

And fill it full of pleasant cliches
like 'God is love' and 'heaven is above',
and, believe it or not, earth is below,
and we will all let love work.

And don't mention anything like sin
or have words like death and destruction creeping in.
Do not discuss spirituality
or good and evil and their duality,
because these days we are all too ignorant
to have a sensible debate about religion
but say words like humble and downtrodden,
because after all this hymn is modern.

Make me a modern Christian song
and one that you can strum along to
on your guitar or bang your bongo drum
because it looks good on *Songs of Praise,*
and in the middle put in plenty of surprises
just in case we are all falling asleep.

Make me a modern Christian song
and one that is twelve minutes long
so if you forget the words then you can hum,
dum di dum, God is our chum
and that is why we have come to church.

Lloyd Evans

What they said:

'He was six feet tall' Joseph Conrad
'Ridden with lice' Julian Barnes
'I've never heard of him' Jarvis Cocker
'Once again a major artist has emerged' New Statesman
'Human, all too human' Friedrich Nietzsche
'Magnifique' Gustave Flaubert
'We want Barabas! . . . The People of Israel

Hey! Hey! – Pinochet!

Hey Pinochet – your holiday
Is over – what a pity.
That bargain break was a big mistake
In the world's coolest city.

But hey – hey Pinochet
Lots of people in the UK
Reckon some of the things you did
Were just about OK.

You were good for Chile's economy
You put it back on the rails.
You turned empty football stadiums
Into thriving jails.

You were a modern tyrant
You never used whips or chains.
You rounded up your rivals
And plugged them into the mains.

But all those people vanishing
That was a wicked, shameful thing
It means that you're responsible
For all those songs by Sting.

Then halfway through your bloody career,
You did something strange.
You held a referendum
And the people wanted change.

But hey – hey – Pinochet –
You're a fool – you had it made,
Elections are there to be rigged
They shouldn't be obeyed.

If you're a ruthless autocrat
That's not how things are done.
You're supposed to cling to power for years
Then hand it on to your son.

But hey – hey – Pinochet
The word is – you're not well.
And the ghosts of all your victims
Are awaiting your death knell
And testing all the plug sockets
In your infernal cell.
And the bad news is there's never been
A power cut in hell.

Advice to Mothers

Beat your children black and blue,
Beat them with an iron will.
Beat them when you've things to do,
Beat them when you've time to kill.

Thrash them with a snooker cue
Hit them with a cricket bat
Have you got a didgeree-doo?
Well have a go with that.

Children these days, it's no wonder
That you beat them in the bath.
And while you hold their dear heads under
Don't feel guilty if you laugh.

Give your kids a daily creaming.
Or Next Door will start to say,
'I can't hear those children screaming.
Hope the parents are OK.'

Beat the children, oh beat them
Especially when their crimes are trivial.
Pour yourself some olives, eat them.
Make the whole thing more convivial.
Pick a favourite from your brood.
Let him think you like him best
When he's in triumphant mood
Beat him harder than the rest.

Beat the children, oh beat them.
Beat their little bones to rubble.
Beat them, yes, but don't eat them
Or you'll find yourself in trouble.

When the Child Inspectors knock
To ask about the dreadful noise,
Hand the cue-ball in a sock
Say 'Do the girls, I've done the boys.'

Beat the children, oh beat them.
Always have those big hands ready.
Beat them when they come home early
Because they want to play with teddy.
Beat them for being girly.
Even if they're girls already.

There's a lot of twaddle spoken
By the Left who seem to feel
That with bodies, minds are broken
And the scars will never heal.
Take Prince Charles, thrashed and beaten
Buggered stiff at Gordonstoun,
But he did all right at Eton,
Now he's the heir to the throne.

Beat the children, oh beat them.
When the Liberals tell you – 'Look.
You damage kids the way you treat them.
Here's the evidence in this book.'
Settle the dispute with grace,
Take the hardback, have a look,

Then smash them with it in the face
And follow with the old right hook.

Yes beat the Liberals oh, beat them.
Turn their evidence on its head.
It's the best way to defeat them.
Thrash them with it till they're dead.

When the public gallery's leering
And the judge has just read out your fate
And asks to know in the court's hearing
What inspired this reign of hate.
Be coquettish, touch an ear-ring,
Say your book on Child Rearing
Was a little out of date.

Beat the children, oh beat them.
Even in your prison cell.
Find a chance, rack your brains.
Ask to bid your kids farewell.
Then beat them, beat them with your chains.

And when they let you out on licence,
Fake a CV, dye your hair,
And with muscles hard as Tyson's
Get a job as an au pair.

Poem About A Man Whose Wife Leaves Him For Good

I wish to God you hadn't died two days into our
    honeymoon,
Because your parents and my Dad will want grandchildren
    soon.
You always were dead gorgeous, and you're still gorgeous
    dead,
I wish I'd had you buried but it's lonely in my bed.
And Katy you're so lovely I spend each night in tears
Snuggling beside you, nibbling leaf mould from your ears
And doing other things for which I'd get at least five years.

I wish your parents wouldn't ask themselves around to
    dinner:
Your mother sitting grumbling saying 'Katy's getting
    thinner.'
And your father, knocking back my wine, with
'Why's she gone so quiet?'
I wish I didn't have to say, 'She's on a special diet
Which makes her want to talk less. Why don't you two
    try it?'

I wish when *we* invited friends you'd be a bit less frigid.
And stop your body language saying 'You all bore me
    rigid.'
I wish at cocktail parties you'd network a little harder.
But you're always in the kitchen, propped against the
    larder.
When our house was on the market I wish you'd stayed in
    place,

But you keeled out of the closet, and hit the buyer in the face.
And when his heart had been restarted he'd lost interest in
    the place.

I wish your rotting innards hadn't made your stomach swell,
So my Dad gave you a slap and said. 'She's pregnant
I can tell.'

I wish I hadn't humoured him by taking up the option
Of pretending we're a loving couple eager for adoption.
I felt certain Hackney Council would exclude us from the
    shortlist,
On the grounds that you were dead. But they said
'Well, let's not be corpsist.'

I wish they'd sent a boy who was perhaps a little older
And hadn't gripped your arm so tight it snapped off at the
    shoulder.
And when the lad grows up I hope he'll break the family
    tradition,
Of placing our dead around the house in an
    eye-catching position.
Like my mother in the lounge between the van Gogh and
    the Titian.
And Auntie Jean with Uncle Pete in the room where he
    first wooed her.
Rolled against the skirting board as a human draught
    excluder.

I wish to God, if nothing else, when he's a man he learns
To honour and obey my Will which states in graphic terms:
'Burn me, bury me at sea or feed me to the worms.'

Martina Evans was born in 1961 and grew up in Co. Cork. She trained as a radiographer at St Vincent's Hospital, Dublin, and moved to London in 1988. Her first collection of poems, *The Inniscarra Bar and Cycle Rest*, appeared in 1995 (Rockingham Press). She is also the author of two novels, *Midnight Feast* (Vintage, 1996) and *The Glass Mountain* (Vintage, 1997).

The Pet

It's a tonic to see you, so it is, now I mean that.

James hardly ever talks about you and I'm mad to know
   everything.

It's all Grainne with him. Didn't you know? Oh god, yes.

Grainne this, Grainne that, Grainne's extension, Grainne's
   operation.

That's not fair, to you. I mean that. Is it now?

To treat your children like that, now, my heart goes out to
   you.

Going on about the one child the whole time.

Going back and back to the one child, like a boomerang
   gone wallop.

Every one of my grandchildren (and I've got eleven of
   them) gets the same present every Christmas.

Four pound ninety nine pence worth of something, and I
   have to be cute about it.

They're watching like hawks the whole time.

What did Diarmuid get? What did Sara get? What! What!
   What!

How much, how much, four pound ninety-nine pence.

Sometimes I do have to go over and above.

Donal doesn't like cheap things for the children and you
    can't blame him.
Isn't the whole world smothering under plastic?
The girls are the worst, though. They're like foxes.
They say Donal is my pet and he's getting the pub.
Isn't he the only boy?
They're like hens fighting in the yard.
They say, well, I suppose he is my only boy, that I'm
partial, but I can't cut the business into five pieces, can I?
But I am really, a small biteen partial, he is my one and
    only, he *is* my favourite.

Andy Fairley, a hero of the West Country avant-garde, is currently seated at the right hand of his celestial muse, having 'done died and gone to heaven' in 1999.

Jack The Biscuit

HE WAS BORN IN 1964
IN THE MENTAL HOME WE CALLED NEXT DOOR
DILUTING HIS INSANITY WITH POCKET MIRROR
   VANITY
AND BEER AND WINE BUT NEVER MULLED
ALWAYS SURE HIS MIND WAS DULLED
HIS GAZE WAS STRAIGHT AND ALWAYS BLURRED
HIS BRAIN WAS SHAKEN BUT NEVER STIRRED
HE SAW HIS BUDDIES FADE AWAY
WITHIN A YEAR OR JUST A DAY
'SUCK ON THIS' HE SEEMED TO SAY
AND NEVER TOOK HIS FIST AWAY
AND LATER ON WITHIN THIS VOID
HE KNOCKED ABOUT OR JUST DESTROYED
A FOOTBALL SLOGAN ON HIS LIPS
HE SWAGGERED ROUND WITH LEADEN HIPS

ONCE HE HAD BROKEN OFF THE LEASH
HE'D FIND A CLUB OR SHADY NICHE
HE TOOK NO LIP, NO SHIT, NO QUARTER
HARD CURRENCY OR ALL OUT SLAUGHTER
THEN FOUND A GIRL OR RATHER BOUGHT HER
MARRIED, DIVORCED AND HAD A DAUGHTER

HE WAS ALWAYS QUICK FOR PROPHECIES
'WHERE THE FIST DON'T WORK THERE'S ALWAYS
  KNEES,
IT'S A FOOT IN THE DOOR OR IN THE GROIN
MY CLUB'S EXCLUSIVE, YOU CAN'T JOIN,'
WAS JACK'S WISE WORDS HE SAID TO ME
WHILE LIVING IN HIS FANTASY
EXISTING IN A STATE OF TENSION
TILL FALLING BACK ON EARLY PENSION
KICKING A BALL TILL OUT OF BREATH
THE BALL HIS LIFE, HIS FOOT WAS DEATH

WHAT IT WAS, HE COULDN'T WEAR IT
DRANK ALL THE MORE TO GRIN AND BEAR IT
NO TIME, NO SPACE, OR ROOM TO SHARE IT
JACK THE BISCUIT.

'Hell's Angels don't scare me,' says Hastings-born **Salena Saliva Godden**. 'If you can booze with heavily tattooed, hardcore fishermen, you're fixed for anything.'

She is the product of a 'mad artist mother' and a family that wouldn't shut up. 'If you were quiet for more than twenty seconds in my household then they thought there was something wrong with you. If I was writing or reading then that was deemed OK and I would be left alone. I think I started writing for some peace and quiet.' Salena recently started her own imprint, Saltpetre, with Peter Coyte.

To The Man With The Hair

He had big, brown,
Bushy,
Curly hair,
He looked like the one with curly hair,
In Starsky and Hutch,
But,
Pale,
Pink,
With glass,
Blue,
Irish eyes.

He was critical,
Cold,
Sharp like a razor.

He loved discipline,
Loved it,
He loved dishing it out,

Demanding obedience,
Putting his foot down,
With a firm hand,
That he did love.

He'd have had to have,
Otherwise,
He wouldn't be in this poem.

My old stepfather,
You cruel, unkind, bastard,
I hear you are bald now.

TV Ladies

Now I know who I want to be.
That lady on my TV
I know that I want to be the lady on my TV
You've all seen her,
So you know what I am saying,
I don't know how she does it?
Or what card she's playing?
What God she's paying?

As she goes up the iron-gated elevator,
The opening credits roll up the screen,
The sax lilts then softens like butter,
In this butterkist popcorn dream scene.
The camera zooms around the gorgeous warehouse
    apartment,

Spacious, white and airy, she lives there alone,
Perhaps a rabbit or a kooky cockatoo,
A palatial residence where she lives on her own.

Although in the movie she is a struggling cellist,
Or she works in a small and funky bookstore,
But rent and money just don't exist,
All huge windows, gaping balcony and polished wooden
    floor.
She opens one of the windows, sunsetting,
Breathtaking view of the city, breathing to night,
She kicks off her Prada heels and stockings,
Barefoot on the varnished wood, dancing muslin white.

Her groceries in the open-plan kitchen, the brown paper
    bag,
Full of fresh cool veg, fruit and ice-cream,
Camera to close-up as she spoons lazily to mouth,
Have you seen this movie? Have you had this dream?
Anyway, that's who I want to be,
The lady at the start of every TV movie,
Somehow financially secure aged under and about 32,
Eating chinese from a white box, you know, like they do.

Now, I am not saying I want to be American,
Sharon Stone, Cheryl Ladd, Bridget Fonda or even
    Courtney Cox,
But they do make grey yale sweatshirts, rolled–down white
    socks,
Look kind of sporty, in control, even sexy on the box.
The downside (apart from the sax player) is that they have
    to witness a murder,

Or find a body and spend the next hour and a half on the
    run,
Or they accidentally tap into a secret FBI e-mail,
Or they get framed, their fingerprints found on the gun.

And they always have basketball nets attached to their wall,
Which they'll drop a ball through, waiting for a call,
From the Detective Superintendent to warn her the serial
    killer's at the door.
Or he'll be the psycho killer who hates struggling cellists
    and the local bookstore.
Now, sometimes the lady is unfortunately blind and in the
    love scene will say,
'Am I beautiful' in an endearing, boss-eyed, shagging the
    murderer type way.
As the rabbit or the cockatoo boils away at gas mark 3,
Oh yes, that's who I want to be, the lady on my TV

Christopher Walken, tapes you talkin',
Whilst Kevin Spacey, sniffs your lacys,
Rutger Hauer, films you in the shower,
Brad Pitt, use your imagination.
Oh! You've seen the movie 100 times or more,
The fantastic vunerable siren on the 42nd floor,
The one who stubs out cigarettes after only one pull,
Because the actress doesn't really smoke or some other
    bull.

The one who doesn't take a torch to the no-lights
    basement,
And what she was doing going down there anyway, is
    anyone's missed clue,

And never saying goodbye on the telephone,
Have you noticed how they do that too?
Bah! I take it back now, I don't want to be,
That stupid lady on my TV movie.
Falling over when chased by axe-wielding psychotic,
Sex with the good, bad, good, cop with fruits all exotic,
Playing cello like I invented erotic,
With my TV tears, my Freudian fears,
My Oscar-winning toned and tender thighs,
Now, I'm telling lies,
I lie, I would die, if I had just one chance,
I want to wake up and be the lady in Flashdance,
What a feeling!

Roy Harper is considered to be one of the most influential song-writers of his generation and to have inspired such musicians as Led Zeppelin, Pink Floyd, David Bowie, Jethro Tull and more recently Damon Albam of Blur. Roy has recorded over thirty albums and has collaborated with Jimmy Page, Kate Bush and David Gilmour amongst many others.

As everyone knows, Roy has lived a hell of a life and continues to tour. A biography isn't too far away.

Lunchtime Sandwich Secretaries

Poured together into disco
98.6 am
kitted out in suits of armour
amorous in future glow
pointed brassierey winkle
pickers In the poppy cock
together sprouting at the wrinkle
Monday morning mirror shock

Lunchtime sandwich secretaries
bustle in the cheese and pickle
hunt in packs and wolf the whistle
Lamborghini daydream boys
soon to be remembering
with sticks and faded aspiration
safe beyond the mid-life crisis
rungs of slippy fingering

Thousands millions in the shakeup
making out on seismic faults
sensual plagues st. vitus dancing

silver paper toothpaste megavolts
power up the engineering
full of beans at every stage
fill the genes with euthanasia
anything except old age

Stop! Enough!
next generation
step into the dingbat cave
carnal romping
major nation
new jog jigging jarring rave

Nero

Upstairs
There's a room
Upstairs
Where a man
Tries to leave
But slowly
The door's become
Part of the wall
And the windows
Are hard to believe

Downstairs
A sensuous
Carnal fool
Connives
Indulges the role

There was more
But I was fiddling

Fay Hart was born in Ireland and raised in the backwoods of Indiana. At the age of fourteen she moved to Florida with her family where she dropped out of school and began a journey across America, working at a variety of jobs while recording her adventures in a series of self-published poetry booklets.

Since moving to London she has collaborated with different artists combining poetry with music, photography and film. Her work with filmmaker Vivienne Dick, '3AM', a visual poem commissioned for the BBC Late Show, was chosen for the ICA Biennial in 1993 and more recently included in the International Festival, Sao Paulo. She's also worked with photographer Brian Griffin, and was a founder member of Steve Nieve's notorious Deep End Club.

My Great Life

This is my great life.
It bears no resemblance to
your mistrustful glance
nor your words – lurching,
drunk on their own poison,
altering the moodswing of
my kitchen.
Your haute couture fleece
shedding laborious threads
that bind into elaborate
carpets
and underneath –
a skin, stinging with insults.
I am sewing white curtains to the
cracks in the walls
and delivering handfuls of blue

shells of eggs
to the ends of the beds.
I am holding up the sky
& weaving great mountains of heartache
and hair from the drain
into phenomenal hearts
that I hang from the door.
This is my great life
& your indignation cannot
come here anymore.

Riot Girl

She was a riot girl I once knew
Didn't let nobody tell her what to do
She defied her daddy she defied her god
She defiled her body with a boy named Bob
She rode a Honda Super90 and red
Had dayglow hair & was good in bed
She was a riot girl don't you know
One day she met a guy called Dan
Sure enough, he was going to be her man
They thought they would get it right
Raising babies was going to be delightful
She charmed her way to school
Broke every goddamn rule
She let them sleep on the roof
Eat from the floor
If the babies wanted honey
she just gave them more

She was a riot girl I once knew
Wouldn't let nobody tell her what to do
But the dad got scared one day
And he just up and ran away
She started heading for the door herself
Stopped, paused once and decided she'd stay
She was a riot girl after all
She said I'll raise these babies on my own
Even now they was half-way grown
Then she heard it on a car radio —
A woman singing about a man who wants to go
And when she heard the words in the song
She knew he wasn't really wrong
So she called him on a telephone
She said I ain't angry that you left me on my own
And then she sang;
'If you're weak enough to leave me
I'm strong enough to let you go'
She was a riot girl I once knew.

Better Drinker

Act like a lady he said
Hell, I'm more of a man than you'll ever hope to be
I retorted,
He wanted to take me to California,
Co-dependants in a dysfunctional bar.
We sat drink to drink, thigh to thigh, rock-n-rye,
You bet I'll try anything on offer.
& at the sound of the bell
that signals the barman's got better things to do,
my heart screams the Salty Dog Lounge –
they got another hour there because it's on the county line.
It'd take half an hour to get there he reminds
and stomps off mad as hell.
I'm a better drinker than you.
I point that Chrysler to the county line
and wake up on a rusty boxspring
with one of them better drinkers.
And now with this warm bathwater
I am trying to deflect
the shards of hangover & anonymous sex.

PJ Harvey – songwriter, singer, musician, actress, visual artist – is acknowledged as one of Britain's most respected and consistently groundbreaking creative forces. Her starkly original recordings and compelling live shows have brought critical acclaim on both sides of the Atlantic.

Since 1991 she has released five albums, collecting three nominations each in the Mercury, Brit and Grammy awards. Her two most recent albums, *To Bring You My Love* and *Is This Desire?*, have each won album of the year accolades internationally.

Side projects have included a collaboration with John Parish to provide music for the Mark Bruce Dance Company's *Dance Hall at Louse Point* and contributions to records by Nick Cave, Tricky and Pascal Comelade. She has written soundtrack music for films including *Basquiat*, *Stella Does Tricks* and *Batman Forever*. Meanwhile, Polly made her acting debut as Mary Magdalene in Hal Hartley's 1998 movie, *The Book of Life*. She is also an accomplished visual artist and has exhibited her sculpture, photography and drawings in various UK galleries.

STONED

GREY
FUCKED OFF
NOT AT HOME
HARD BLUE EYES
STONED
STONED
STONED

LESS OF AN OPEN WOUND

One Line

I long for you,
You, whom I destroyed.
I yearn for you.
My heart pressed up against my head.
Shallow-breathing.
The feeling,
Still sends me racing.

I draw a line.
A thread across the rolling country
To the crushed city.
Your lightened window to mine.
Right here, right now, this time of day,
As light and stars come into play,
Your head,
In mine.
Your heart.
One line.

Born in Clermiston in 1961, **Davy Henderson** makes up one fifth of The Nectarine No. 9. He also plays with Black Paint.
Currently making up '(sic)' for The Nectarine No. 9 and 'can this be invisibly mended said the holey ghost' for The Measurement of Souls.
Likes: fake eyelashes.

Tape Y/r Head On

I read the mind of jesus
i got it second-hand
down the st johns road
at some charity stand

i hang around the garden
eatin' dirty fruit
what's this
inspiration
i bought it from
st james's underground
carboot

why are the trees so big
then
why are the leaves
so green
why did you ever leave me
then
where on earth y'been

tape it
tape y/r head on

bless y/r son
w/ovaltine
make a great home-movie
kickin bread all around
the lawn
i never felt so groovy
tape it
tape y/r head on

i read the mind of jesus
i bought it
second-hand
down the st johns rd . . .

Damien Hirst is an artist. **Joe Strummer** is a musician.

This poem was born on Tuesday 6 Oct 1998 and floated on the Internet. They met at Womad in 1996 and have been great friends ever since. Damien says:

'I was lying by a fire, on the ground at Womad and he (Joe) put a pillow under my head and covered me with a duvet at 4.00 in the afternoon after I'd drunk too much, smoked too many spliffs and taken too much Charlie. I fell in love with him.'

Jimmy Clitheroe's Penis

Christmas lights and
poncy baubles,
cannot make a sparrow warble.
You cunt, you shit, you
pig from hell,
you leech,
you ghoul,
you fantasy vaudeville.

Adam Horovitz was born in London in 1971 and bred in Gloucestershire. He is a slam-winning poet who has performed in numerous venues, including the Cheltenham Literature Festival and Glastonbury Festival. In 1996, he took part in the first Slovenian Festival of Poetry and Wine, which he maintains is an almost perfect combination.

He is a member of the Stroud Football Poets and runs 'Hoo-Hah' (Poetry in Commotion). He has worked as a theatre usher, silver-service waiter, sheep dipper, barman, journalist, radio DJ and bouncer; but has always returned to poetry because it involves more exercise.

Burials

I remember you telling me — assured in bar-room confidence —
of a burial years ago in Elcombe woods up at the high point,
the stony point, where the local workmen, chewing their
    cud of cider,
refused to work. They told the husband that his wife would
    get no further
down than three feet, you said, although the grave was
    eventually dug.

You seemed astonished, and questioned the sanctity of such
    an act,
siding in Protestant horror with the old rogues buried in
    their pints
who mix and match their myths to suit the night.
You closed off when I told you I had dug the grave
with the family of the deceased two years before;
had stood, at six foot four, shoulder deep in consecrated
    earth
carving a chronicle of love into the tablet hill.

It was as if I disappointed you, gave you a truth you did
    not need,
intruding on your excitement with a pick and spade.
I apologise. All stories are true; I know that now.
Unwritten memories and bodies subside like pit villages,
abandoned and consumed by the slag of yesterday, today,
    tomorrow,
but they leave small spaces where poppies and dandelions
    grow
amongst resurgent grass. All burials are beginnings.

At This Time

Statistics not available.
Plans and applications not available.
Photocopied reports from bloody depths of bureaucracy
not available.
Orchards not available.
Aspirin not available
Pleasant valley walks not available.
Childhood available elsewhere.

Sunday school not available.
Imagination not available.
Cider presses not available.
Big dogs with grotty noses
not available.
Kissing gates not available.
Beer not available.
Reporters only available if beer available.

Books not available.
Economists not available.
Bare-footed taxmen no longer available.
Miffed of Miserden not available.
Sculptors not available.
Cowslips not available.
Pools to drown in not available.
Sewage and concrete available always
if price is right.

Prices not available.
Wallets not available.
Poets and anarchists not available
except for lecture tours in far countries
with big wars.
England wicket keepers not available.
Trees not available.
Sunsets not available.
Badgers not available unless peanuts paid for.
Bungalows available at all times.

Pig-farmers not available.
Sheep not available.
Locals not available for comment or otherwise.
Telephones available, but not as available as vandals.
Chaffinches not available.
Torches not available or necessary.
Bicycles not available.
N.C.P. car park available on old pub site.

BBC film crews and other archaeologists available.
Holographic Laurie Lee available.

Midsummer morning traffic-log available.
Small chunks of Cotswold stone available.
Mortgages available.
Rustic 1930s charm available
from staff of three storey theme restaurant
on request.
Chartered helicopter flights available.
Genuine gravestones available.

'Cider with Disney' available.
Sex in aforementioned bungalows available.
Prices available for that.

Prime Minister available for facile speeches
about importance of countryside
and visits from Presidents.
Jilly Cooper available.
Jilly Cooper available.

Explosives not available.

At
this
time.

MC Jabber, a.k.a. Scott Martingell, was born in Croydon and lives in Huddersfield. In 1995 he won the UK Poetry Slam Championship. Tall and lanky, he has been called 'a gibbering poetic genius'.
He specialises in word salad, freaky hip-hop, and is a word rapper.

Dust

Sad man, I'm so introspective. My own perspective is just too subjective. I'm losing respect; I reject my own intellect. Trying to inject a little extra effect. I'm losing faith in my ability to put it down. I'll take off the crown – it's too heavy, and I'll set it down. Eliminate meaning, enunciate the special sound – the sound between words, between sound, when it all breaks down.

Defined with a rhyme, cos it's the only time I can find a structure. Pulling you into my deep throat, and you'll find I've sucked ya dry as a bone, dry as a mouth, dry as the desert sun. Dry as the world inside your head, where you're the only one for miles and miles and miles and miles and miles around – the sound between words, between sound, when it all breaks down.

Pull on the glove, the reality is virtual. Open wide your mind – it's gonna hurt; you'll wish you had a god you could believe in – something that makes it easier when you're leaving. Something that eases the pain of your departure, something that gives the finish to the start; you're looking for something won't diminish your demeaning – the end, the death, the finish of all your meaning. Pull on the glove, feel the pressure points touch. You can live on, the virtual is such a tempting choice, rejoice in the sedative, the kind of voice that whispers an alternative.

When you die, it doesn't have to be dust. There must be something else cos there must be something else, there must be something. Pull on the glove and make yourself sing. There must be some deeper meaning to life. There must be some reason for all this strife. There must be some reason to say 'must.' When you die it doesn't have to be dust.

Press your face into a Mandelbrot set. See the way that the patterns interesect. Feel the way that their similarity mirrors your own in its particularity. Lie on a death-bed – peculiarity – doing a Huxley, taking LSD – 'I don't like that wallpaper, you know; sooner or later, one of us has gotta go'.

I slip on the glove – it's waiting for me – a virtual, almost real reality, and if I close my eyes I might find one as real as the one I left behind. One whose contours, like a map of my soul, open me up and leave me with a hole. A god-shaped hole, the shape of my brain. Open me up, in flames and in pain. That's why I've got the bottle to do this. Anyone fancy trying to take the piss? Trying to drag themselves to their feet?

Fuck the rhymes, I'll cut you in the street. I'll take a knife and open up a vein; a God-shaped hole, the shape of my brain. Don't make a date you can't keep. There must be something deep, something deep.

When you die, it doesn't have to be dust. There must be

something else cos there must be something else, there must be something. Pull on the glove and make yourself sing. There must be some deeper meaning to life. There must be some reason for all this strife. There must be some reason to say 'must'. When you die it doesn't have to be dust.

Pull on that virtual reality glove round my head, till I think I've had enough. Close the material around my face, so when I die you can take me to a place where death and entropy don't exist; where the only life is a mystery, you feel that none of it's real. Sooner or later will come a time that we'll lie on our backs and see the stars wheel over our heads, faster than we can feel. A minute, a second, a second, an hour, speeded up like an opening flower. Throwing its colours outward to the sun; then, like a film, as soon as it's begun, it withers and closes back to nothing.

There must be something, something. When you die, it doesn't have to be dust. There must be something else cos there must be something else, there must be something. Pull on the glove and make yourself sing. There must be some deeper meaning to life. There must be some reason for all this strife. There must be some reason to say 'must'. When you die it doesn't have to be dust.

If you strain your eyes to the distance, you might see my dust. I don't even need to count the syllables, cos I can trust my instinct and judgement for style and form implicitly. I don't need to think of the content — it comes naturally.

When I was a kid, I used to look under my bed at night, but now that fright is my delight, cos I embrace the fight. The only thing bigger than my fear is my eternal rage, structured and exorcised through eyes and pen and page.

You wanna be taught that thought is unnecessary – you can't even imagine a challenge to your authority – you gotta work at arrogance; it don't come easily. If you can't get it up, get down, cos you can't get with me. Why are you even bothering? It's a waste of ink. Who am I talking to – you or me? – Well, what d'you think?

Your starter for ten, think carefully, and take your time, and I'll just be here, anticipating and creating rhyme. I'll just be waiting here, giving advice, like: iodine for lice; get a cat if you've got mice; having sex with a woman with a cold is pretty nice, cos when she coughs – *man!* – it's like a vice!

I'm hot like ice, cold as the undying flame. There's a J and an ay, a double bee, an ee ar in my name, cos 'to Jabber' is 'to drivel and dribble' (like you're out to lunch), but a 'Jabber's' also 'someone who jabs' (with a lethal punch). Choosing my moment, then I strike with deadly accuracy. Sparring with you or your shadow, it's all the same to me. You wanted to know how it's really done, so you came to me – if you can't get it up, get down, cos you can't get with me. If you can't gee-ee-tee eye-tee you-pee, get dee-oh-double-you-en, cos you can't get with me. If you can't gee-ee-tee-eye-tee you-pee, get dee-oh double-you-en, cos you can't get with me.

With a pee and an oh, an ee em, we're together again. I'm just the same as you – I don't know whether a pen will constrain my insane brain; will it contain my flame? Will it explain, inflame my frame as I make it plain in words of just one ess why double-ell-ay-bee-ell-ee; *va te faire foutre, figli putana* and *do prdele*; I've got 24 languages at my fingertips.

There ain't no slips between the microphone, my hand, my lips. I don't spill a drop. I fill you up to overflowing. We're flowing. We're exchanging fluids. I'm showing you how to pause, how to go s-l-o-w-l-y. If you can't get it up, get down, cos you can't get with me.

If you can't get it up, if you can't get it hard, then your rhymes are plastic, man, just like a credit card. I think I'll finish, though I could go on for an eternity – if you can't get it up, get down, cos you can't get with me. If you can't gee-ee-tee eye-tee you-pee, get dee-oh double-you-en, cos you can't get with me. If you can't gee-ee-tee eye-tee you-pee, get dee-oh-double-you, get dee-oh-double-you, get dee-oh-double-you-en, cos you can't get with me.

Alan Jenkins was born in 1955 in London, where he has lived ever since, apart from three years at the University of Sussex and a year spent in France and Greece. Early promise as an R&B singer and a women's agony aunt was not fulfilled, so for the past fifteen-odd years he has worked at the *TLS*, where he is Deputy Editor. He has published three books of poems, all with Chatto and Windus: *In the Hot-house* (1988), *Greenheart* (1990) and *Harm*, which won the Forward Prize for Best Collection in 1994. A fourth volume, *The Drift*, is due in 2000, bugs permitting.

Rio Song

I was settled in a likely-looking bar
drinking caipirinhas chased by beer
when a dark voice whispered in my ear
    No money, no honey.

She was sixteen if she was a day,
she wore a black thing like a bustier
her black eyes looked at me as if to say
    No money, no honey.

Her thin hand stroked my thigh, my crotch,
my wrist, and lingered on my watch;
she leaned back, ordered double scotch —
    No money, no honey.

She drank and told me I should go out back
where on a mattress covered by a sack
she'd take my mind off its one track:
    No money, no honey.

She'd ease my body too, she swore
she'd do what I told her to and more
but this was the rule for rich and poor:
   No money, no honey.

'My brother deals, my mother begs'
(she stretched out, stroked her naked legs)
'I'm not going to end up with the dregs:
   No money, no honey.'

The air was heavy with the coming storm
my shirt was soaked, she was merely warm
my head buzzed like an angry swarm –
   No money, no honey.

She cupped her breasts, she gestured at the door
cascasa streamed from every pore
the samba throbbed, by now I knew the score
   No money, no honey.

I checked my wallet. Checked my keys.
I thought of you back home, thought of disease.
She was already talking to a Japanese:
   No money, no honey.

The Road Less Travelled

I've never scaled the heights of Macchu Picchu with a
    backpack
or trekked through India, breakfasting on hunger,
or listened in the African night to the insects' claptrap,
smoked a peace-pipe on Big Sur, or surfed Down Under.

I never featured on the cork board in your kitchen
among the postcards from the friends who'd gone to Goa,
Guatemala, Guam; among the glossy shots of lichen-
and liana-festooned temples, girls who grin *Aloa!*

I never wrote, 'I have walked the sands of Dar-es-Salaam
and seen elephants drink from the great Zambezi';
'Moving on to Bogota', 'Babar says *Salaam*
from San Francisco', 'Here in Maui the living's easy'.

(I always sent my greetings from a café, *camera* or *chambre*
with a view of the Rose Window, Bridge of Sighs,
    Alhambra . . .)

But if I stand on my rooftop in London West Eleven
with my head in the clouds of Cloudesley Place, North
    One
I can get it clear: how one day you'll move earth and
    heaven
to have me here, but I'll have changed tack, I'll be gone

in search of some more fascinating place or person,
I'll have made a fresh start, with no thought, now, of
    failure,
it won't be my emotions that you play on (or rehearse on),
it won't be my tongue that tastes the coastline of Australia

in the birthmark on your thigh; it won't be me who brings
    you
tea in bed, or a cappuccino with the froth still on it,
or performs my 'Dance to Morning' for you, or sings you
'The Shadow of your Smile', or writes a double sonnet

to you, to your freckled breasts, your sturdy
dancer's legs and neat behind (or, if that's too wordy

for your answering machine, ghazals
to your eyes that are the colour of the clear green water
of Sardinia), or puts on 'El cant dels ocells' by Casals
and holds the phone up to the speaker, or holds your
    daughter
to the sunrise in a suburban garden with galahs
and kookaburras, holds her up as if I'd caught her
to hear the song of the Catalan birds, and Bala's.

Patrick Jones was born in 1965 in Tredegar, South Wales. He had a happy, idyllic childhood of fields, swifts, stars and muddy football pitches. After attending Oakdale Comprehensive school, Cross Keys College and Swansea University, he has worked in over forty different jobs – however, his vocation is writing.

He lives quietly in Blackwood with Catherine and their four children – Rebekah, Evan, Ethan and Victoria – and believes that poetry should lick the soul.

manscape

blue unsky blue tv scatters solitudes across the silent
   streets. lamps stutter stutter
light into darkness; valley darkness; valley coal choked mind
   stabbed wounds of
night.night.night.fear as necessity.manacled.man.teenagers in
   building society
doorways; kick it down; kick it down.doorways.doorways
   doorways.such exits are
unknown to stars
stars.sadnesses unspoken forever buried beneath alcohol
and pride.hole hole.dog shit on concrete.aloneness in
crowds.larynx laceration.emancipation.e man.man. e.e. e.
e.all speech is useless.stab the silence with blood.make it
taste real.feel real.feel.make it sing like
chapel.chapel.nothing.no thing moves.tiny houses.flicker
screen.tv.freedom.satellite dishes devour,devour art like
mankind.your last day.your last
day.last.your.day.last.your.day.is.it.it is.is.is.we are
all as invisible as air.liposuction can only remove what was
   never
there.saturday.freedom.tv.saturday.everyday.lottery.love.death.

life.live.noel edmonds houseparty.party.black
sky.starshine.black streets.black night.tv.tv.light.light.
everything must go;

Anima Mundi–World Soul

As i sit down to write about the now about wales about
  the assembly
about politics it's strange as whatever angle attracts me the
  word
kosovo appears – in black – so i felt that whatever i wrote
  about, that
word, which could, as when aneurin bevan said, 'the verb
  is more
important than the noun,' now be taken as a verb – a post
  post-modern
word to denote some hideous crime against humanity – all
  my other
thoughts and ideas seem to crumble into grey as red takes
  over my
landscape – i was going to call it 'land of my fathers what
  have you done
to us' . . . but . . .
here we are, in May, about to embark on a new era –
  yeah – so as the sun
breaks black over the horizon, the leaves turn grey on the
  trees – the
soul waits, the soul waits –
so what are you wales, what are you world?
another statistic, another petalled sympathy another
  bodybag, another

police conference another dead soul rising to the stars
above – another
politician talking of recovery/freedom/off the dole
registers/
democracy/as another life is massacred – wiped out out out
like
sandcastles upon a beach as we watch in our safe homes
through marks
and spencered curtains as we stare at the tv the tv people
as flies settle
on week old babies no mother to cling to no other but the
milk drought
of breasts bleeding from this world's sin and i wish
someone would
cover my eyes and i wish someone would make us see
make us change
all this –
sinn fein fascists serb sadist welsh nationalist
force feeding paramilitary clinging to ideology freedom
without
responsibility necrophilia your calling card
croat serb iraqi   ss
orange men white man belsen gassssss
flags anthems religions
cut up divide destroy deny
all manifestoes breed segregation
all wars intoleration
your violence no redemption
and what do we do – what do we cling to?
new labour plaid cymru raving loony party conservative?
the sweet unadulterated innocence of youth? religion?
politics?

yeah, come on down and save us – paint us a slogan –
    frighten us with
armageddon – crush us through work – whisper gospels of
    consumerism/
hands parrie, throats congeal, language bleeds as bullets rip into
the universal. The universal body that is life that is DEATH.

so as we scream/hide/reach for our credit cards and pray
    for peace, I
stare, searching in the detritus of our lives, furiously
    looking for signs,
for fragments of dignity and meaning and here,
now, a May where the promise of another government
    another border
another division, just feels so wrong and i ask myself what
    has kosovo
got to do with politics, wales, the assembly, this article?
everything, i think, as it probes our apathy, forces us to
    acknowledge our
fragility as humans, makes us realise we are not alone
    pushes us to
believe in something higher than politics, geography, gender
    or religion
something spiritual something born from suffering
and all i can wish for is
the politics of humanity
the economics of equality
the sociology of the soul
and a voice that speaks – stand stand oak tall even the
    smallest body makes a shadow –
from pristina to rwanda from berlin to london from the
    falls road to

chechnya from moscow to lebanon to kosovo and
let it heal the halatosed tongue of our races let it
colour/nation/languageblind and bind us let us lift our eyes
    to the
issues that mean – homelessness, gun control, housing,
    education, health,
poverty, greed, abuse, animal rights and the fucking earth
    but as the
Manic Street Preachers sang— *'bullets for your brain today*
    and we'll forget it all again' . . . I hope we don't . . .
SO FUCK YOU NEW LABOUR A NEW UNIVERSAL
    SOUL IS WHAT WE NEED –
And as i sit down to write i erase the word politics and
    inject the word morality
and as i watch the news my little ones ask me 'why are the
    people are fighting, why are the children are crying'
i reply
'i don't know – just that one group of people didn't like
    another group of people'
'WHY?' comes the reply
'i–i–i don't know' i stammer
they hand me a piece of paper with the word LOVE
    scribbled on it –
'what's that for' i ask
'we're gonna send it to the children, dad'
i close my eyes –
the verb is more important than the noun
i think i'll call this;
'land of my children what can we do for you' . . .

LET POEMS REPLACE GUNS
LET POEMS REPLACE GUNS

(116)

:: Vic Lambrusco

Vic Lambrusco was born in Southampton. He co-founded the
Hard Edge club in Soho with Joe Cairo and ran it from 1989 to 1996.
He was featured on the Misfits CD in 1996.
He writes 'in yer face, politically incorrect' poetry.

Why?

Why is your speech so foul and obscene?
Why d'ya never know what long words mean?

Why d'ya sit indoors and get the horn
Over badly dubbed Scandinavian porn?

Why d'ya eat baked beans from the can
And think Mussolini played for Inter Milan?

Why's your idea of diplomacy
A meeting of Mr. Groin with Mr. Knee?

Why d'ya go out bathed in Aramis
But always come home smelling of curry and piss?

Why d'ya drink lager by the crate?
Why d'ya laugh when your girlfriend's period's late?

And the final question which I have to state
Is why, why, why are you my best mate?

Fran Landesman, born in Manhattan, has lived in London for over thirty-three years. She and her husband Jay Landesman wrote the book and lyrics for *The Nervous Set*, a musical satire on the Beat Generation which opened on Broadway in 1959, starring Larry Hagman as Jack Kerouac and Del Close as Allen Ginsberg. Fran's lyrics have provided material for Barbra Streisand, Ella Fitzgerald, Bette Midler, Shirley Bassey and Chaka Khan amongst others.

Stage productions of her work include *Loose Connections*, *Invade My Privacy*, *Confessions of a Middle-Aged Juvenile Delinquent*. Published collections of her work include *The Ballad of the Sad Young Men and Other Verse* (Polytantric Press, 1975), *Invade My Privacy* (Jonathan Cape, 1978), *The Thorny Side of Love* (Sun tavern fields, 1992) and *Scars & Stripes* (Golden Handshake, 1997).

Fran Landesman is a frequent broadcaster on BBC radio, and has performed on *Loose Ends*, *Kaleidoscope* and *Woman's Hour*, as well as making a guest appearance on *Desert Island Discs*.

An Educated Guess

It seems to me you're flirting with disaster
You're gonna wind up in a mess
I don't have any inside information
That's just an educated guess

You really look sensational this evening
I'm feeling things I can't express
But I'm prepared to hear you say it's over
That's just an educated guess

I don't claim to be clairvoyant
After all I could be wrong

But I've been around a little
And I've heard a lot of songs
Nothing magic lasts for long

I'll probably find someone else to play with
Another beauty in distress
I'll be her friend while trying to forget you
That's just an educated guess

Perhaps when you grow tired of the high life
You may discover more is less
And then you'll see that we belong together
That's just an educated guess
Merely an educated guess

The Usual Suspects

We're somewhere in Soho. The fun never ends.
The usual suspects are what we call friends
The snowbirds are flying
They bitch about art
They spot a new talent and tear it apart

We're scorning the novel and slinging the mud
The scene is reflected in puddles of blood
The resident songbird
Has sung her last lie
The daylight betrays us, It's time for goodbye

The parlour is empty. The punters have fled
The lucky have landed in somebody's bed
And only insiders
Know where, why and when
The usual suspects will gather again
To sneer and conspire
And set hearts on fire again.

If We're So Hip

What did we do with the stuff we had?
We're both so clever. We're both so bad.
Are we beginning to lose our grip?
Why aren't we happy if we're so hip?

We're out of offers. We're out of smoke
I'd like some credit before I croak
It's getting harder to scratch that itch
If we're so clever why aren't we rich?

We watched the great players
Make all the great moves
We know all the patter
Whatever that proves.

Our nice enamel's begun to chip
It may be time to abandon ship
You're always quick with a merry quip
So why aren't we happy
If we're so hip?

This is **Anna Landucci**'s second inclusion in a compilation of poetry, the first being *Random Factor* (Pulp Books). She also has two solo books in print, (*Closing a Past Chapter* and *The Isolation of a Heart*), has written numerous lyrics and is currently working on her first novel. As well as being a writer she is an artist (exhibiting primarily in London and Paris) and singer, having worked with musicians from Massive Attack, Leftfield and Curve.

Post Human

I'm not a real person.
I've made myself up,
stealing identities to make my own.
I'm reinvented to survive the 21st century,
a fabulous invention of one.
I'm Barbie perfect with illusions of tomorrow,
no longer impressed by the electronic dreams.
I've brainwashed away all my history,
so I can be virgin for the next one hundred years.
Speed is my swipe card,
I'm leaving you behind.
I'm leaving this sad century,
off to an irresistible planet
that's more fascinating than earth.
I'm a modern kind of girl wrapped in cellophane,
ready for the last midnight of the millennium.
I'm post human.
You can't touch me,
I'm beyond nature.

Goodbye

The champagne celebration of first desire
is over, it's turned to rust.
This jealousy is eating me alive
taking bites from my heart
and I can't stop it bleeding.
The wasps are swarming again
pushing back the summer fruit sky
until I'm lost in darkness,
lying awake staring at the corners of my bedroom walls.
I would never have suspected you.
I still hear the fully airconditioned sound of your departure,
as your car coolly devoured the motorway
taking you to your new lover
whose face I can only imagine
and wish was drenched with acid.
I wish I could break all clocks
and reverse the time to when we were
happily entwined.
I watch the telephone afraid to dial your number,
knowing you won't answer anyway
but my tongue still burns scalded with goodbye.

Betsy de Lotbinière worked as a journalist for ten years in her hometown, New York, then Rome, Paris and finally in London. It was while interviewing the Mexican film director, Alejandro Jodorowski, that she realised she was in the wrong business. Two children and eighteen-years-with-the-same-man later she writes poetry and fiction. 'Round the Bridging Table' was conceived for a family Christmas in Bridgehampton, New York.

Round the Bridging Table

I
Brothers and Sisters,
Mothers and Daughters,
Fathers and Sons,
Lovers, all,
In the name of Fun:
> The spark and giggle
> Of whim,
Of the Forgetting of Self:
> As the blind leap is made
> Into fiery passion
And the embracing of Rigor:
> The happy sweat of body and
> Mind structuring to realise,
> To manifest
> what it is we most desire
We come together in soulful union.
Everybody say: letting go lets the Spirit in!

II
The egg laid, sat upon,
Chipped by chick
Then feathers grown
(incapable of flight).
Conversations pecked,
Ardour peaked,
Neck chopped,
We eat
This here turkey and
Everybody say: Alleluia! Pass the gravy!

Bread of summer wheat,
Warm winds of picnics,
Ground up to rise,
Bake and pulverise
To reside as stuffing
In turkey
In us.
Everybody say: Mmmmmmm mmmm!

III
Take one argument,
Crack it in a bowl
Of boredom dust.
Melt half a stick of resentment,
Add two cups of defrosted memory
Finely chop:
     Six fistfuls of judgement,
      Three of deceit
And beat.
Cover with a damp cloth of hearsay
Then set the mixture aside.

Roll out the dream dough
(see page 26547 of Life Manual)
Here on that page:
2 Tablespoons of Bath-water
        (preserved at muscle-soothing temperature)
        in which the folly
        of universal smiles was dared,
        connecting all our better selves.
A bombardment of Commercial Powder
        Triggering happy, happy
        Pure and artificial moments
        That show us the way.

Roll out on fantasy board,
Place in Forgiveness Pan
Well-greased with
What-we-want shortening.

In the oven of
Our Mutual Affection
What Has Been filling
Bakes into
What Could Be Crust
        Sweet and sour
        Mingle in
        myths until delicious
What Is pie
Sits before us.
Everybody say: yeah, yeah, let's eat!

IV
Hold hands.
Squeeze hands
Sending jolly possibilities –
Not ignoring the darkness –
But celebrating
The Candlelight Connection.

In the name of
Fun,
Passion,
And Rigor
We come together in the
Soul-fulfilling union of
Love.
Everybody say: letting go lets the Spirit in!

On the evening **Sarah-Jane Lovett** was born, in what was then the Polish city of Pinska, her father went to church and prayed with such intensity that he was locked in all night. Her life after that has never been short of drama. She has witnessed a string of episodes which might have made a lesser spirit cautious or bitter, but in her case have only served to sharpen her courage, her innate sense of adventure, and the resolve to celebrate the world through her poetry. She has two children, Otis and Queenie, and lives in West London.

Trophy Bimbo

A trophy bimbo she shone as
Whilst he was a bit of a catch
And the fact she was half his age
Could not quell this sparkling match

He hid her aside his daughters
But boasted in front of his sons
And winked in a sort of Benny Hill way
When dining out with his chums

Now she's squished into a gruesome Versace
And teeters on Gucci shoes
And enhances her reputation
By being his sexual muse

Oh gorgeous and fresh faced beauty
One look turns him totally numb
And quaintly they josh about the old wife
Who's coolly referred to as 'Mum'.

But goodness her range and her gusto
And goodness those margarine thighs
And goodness the way that she puts it away,
And not once has rumbled those lies.

But shit, now she's talking of babies,
Now that wasn't part of the plan
He's done it already, they're all off his hands
It's a tough life being a man.

Lovey

I'm hoping that my friends will see me me
me at the RSC,
Tonight I'm not performing there
frankly lovey I don't care,
Besides it's nice and cosy here,
and lovely being near the pier.
The matinee's a dodgy one –
be lucky if ten people come,
the evening though we're doing fine
(though half of them are friends of mine).

We were a bit worried at the dress,
the wretched thing was such a mess –
but then of course it always is
everyone's in such a tizz.
The lights were all about the place –
not remotely near my face . . .

Got all the agents to come along,
hopefully they'll like my song –
I put it in especially so
they'll have an idea how far I go
Of course I play the leading part –
the sweetest lamb who breaks my heart
(especially in the kissy scene
that forced removal of the spleen)!

Well, you probably saw me over there,
hovering without a care
Smoozling with the casting folk
(I laugh at everybody's joke).
I'm looking round for who's been in –
Time Out's not it's such a sin,
the INDEPENDENT said they would,
TIMES, they couldn't,
GUARDIAN could –
and so they damn well ought to too
Fucking Shakespeare,
Least mine's new

So . . . let's meet up and have some tea,
and we can maybe talk about me,
And now you can cast me in lots of things,
I'll be waiting . . .
in the wings.

Summer Girl

Is that you my Summer girl?
Battered Start-rites,
Tights not tight enough
Bigger than floss hairdo
Is that you my Summer girl?
I could put you in my pocket
I could dance you through the skies,
You could fit in in-flight luggage,
But that's enough about your size.

Roddy Lumsden was born in St Andrews in 1966. For ten years he made a living of sorts in Edinburgh, mainly by playing quiz machines and working as a quizmaster. He now lives in North London, where he works as a freelance, including writing book reviews and composing word puzzles for newspapers. He received a Gregory Award in 1991 and a Scottish Arts Council bursary in 1994. He was Writing Fellow for the City of Aberdeen in 1995–96 and Selected Poet for The Poetry Society's Poetry Café and website in 1998.

His work first appeared in *Poetry Introduction 8* (Faber & Faber). His first volume, *Yeah Yeah Yeah* (Bloodaxe, 1997), was shortlisted for the Forward and Saltire prizes. His second collection, *The Book of Love*, appears in early 2000.

Acid

My mother told it straight, *London will finish you off,*
and I'd heard what Doctor Johnson said, *When a man is tired of
London, he is tired of life*, but I'd been tired of life

for fourteen years; Scotland, never thoroughly enlightened,
was gathering back its clutch of medieval wonts
and lately there had been what my doctors called a pica

(like a pregnant woman's craving to eat Twix with piccalilli
or chunks of crunchy sea-coal): I'd been guzzling vinegar,
tipping it on everything, falling for women who were

beautifully unsuitable, and hiding up wynds off the Cowgate
with a pokeful of hot chips drenched in the sacred stuff
and wrapped in the latest, not last edition of The Sunday Post

where I read that in London they had found a chardonnay
with a bouquet of vine leaves and bloomed skins, a taste
of grapes and no finish whatsoever, which clinched the deal.

My Pain

(from *Roddy Lumsden is Dead*)

I'm trying to string together three words
which I hate more than I hate myself:
gobsmacked, *hubby* and . . . when I realise
that words no longer count for much at all.

And that's me back down, head on the floor.
It's like Cathal Coughlan goes in his song:
I don't think that I can rise again
till I see how low I can go.

It's like what my ancestors told me in a dream:
You'll be a sponge for the pain of others.
It's like what I said to the local paper lassie:
I do not suffer for my art, I just suffer.

And face it, while we're at it, it's like
what curly Shona said that night at Grafitti
when all the gang were gathered for the show:
how she reckoned I would be the first to die,

or the time I slipped back from the bogs in Bo's
to hear my best friend tell a stranger girl
who'd been sweet in my company, *mind how you go*
with Roddy, he's damaged goods, you know.

Paul Lyalls' verse is a rich mix of comedy, observational therapy and poetical takes on late twentieth-century life – it covers the tennis court of possibilities.

He was born in Goole, East Yorkshire for something he didn't do and makes a regal living from performing at schools, festivals and music gigs.

It's Cool in Goole

Down the Victorian shopping arcade in Goole
20 shops specialising in previously owned
second, third hand, not new – heavily finger-printed-by-time
used gear. Goole's answer to the
Brent Cross and Meadow Hall shopping centres.
I step into the vinyl emporium, disc city,
seven-inch heaven, long playing paradise
a scratchy utopia.
Mind-warping Klaus Wunderlich's
Austrian Tyrol electronic organ
booms around the store – Salzburg ska meets
Blackpool Tower ballroom blitz.
It's run by two men, who, in North London's
Camden Town or New York's East Village
would be called bohemian or eccentric.
In Goole they are called nutters.
Have you got 'All Night Long' by Rainbow
I ask. 'All Night Long' people don't usually
ask for that one, it's usually
'Ever Since You've been Gone'.
A large box marked *headbangin*' is produced.

Single by single is flicked through
violent brain-haemorrhaging anthems
in lurid tasteless sleeves leap into vision
ACDC Twisted Sister, Girlschool,
Poison, Motley Crue the last two being
ponced up boys, big skipping ropes
with pink handles, troweled in cosmetics
in brands and ways not even known to women.
I glimpse Ozzy Osbourne's bared clenched teeth
Joan Jett's eyelashes re-inforced with so much liner
you could have raked leaves with them.
He turns his hand to me, in it is 'All Night Long'.
The sleeve has a standard issue rock siren on it,
crimson dress, industrially-applied make-up
(you could have painted a car quicker)
curves like a Formula One circuit
a real vicar's daughter.
After 4 hours of 'All Night Long' turning constantly
on the family record deck, my mother announces
that she wants to watch Family Fortunes.
But me, suitably fired up head out into the
teeming, maverick heaven-bent-hell-sent Goole night life.
A combination of Casablanca and the last minutes
of the Titanic.
Goole women are great – superbly engineered towering
treats of flesh and fashion with the personalities of
late night TV cabaret-show hosts. Jesus H Christ,
this stunning brunette with a figure that must have
needed planning permission – who could fall into the
North Sea and never drown – legs of a Grand National
winner and a dress that she'd been poured into, but there
had been no one around to say stop – the kind of dress

that lets you know there's plenty more of where
this came from flashes her lashes full on at me.
What would the boys from Rainbow do now?
I wanna touch you, I wanna feel you
I wanna make you mine-ne-ne-ne-ne-iiinneeee.
Twenty minutes later we're back at her place
making it deep and slow into the night
to the sounds of her favourite album
the Greatest Hits of Rainbow.

Shane MacGowan was born on Christmas Day in 1957. He is a singer, songwriter, poet and general *bon viveur*. Kicked out of Westminster School at the age of fourteen, the rest of his life is, as they say, history.

Hands Of The Barmaid

WOTCHAZOMBI
STANDING IN A CROMBIE
LOOKING FOR A TOMBOY
LIKE US, MY FRIEND.
TOOK HIM IN THE JACKS
AND CAME OFF ON HIS BACK.
A DISTANT THANK YOU
MOUTHFUL OF LOVE.
HANDS OF THE BARMAID
JACKING OFF THE WAGE SLAVES
I'M SITTING ON THE FRIDGE
I'M GETTING CLOSE TO THE EDGE
I'M A SENSITIVE PERSON
DRUNK AND BROKE
I'M A POET OF PERVERSION
DYING FOR A POKE
SHE PUTS ANOTHER JAR UP
THEN SHE SHUTS THE BAR UP
NEARLY SMASHED THE CAR UP
WHEN SHE WAS GIVING ME A BLOWJOB.

Pinned Down

FIXED UP
SET UP
SMACKED UP
JACKED UP
SCREWED UP
SPEWED UP
FUCKED UP
LOCKED UP
SITTING THERE IN CHOKEY
FOURTEEN YEARS OLD
NO LOCK ON THE DOOR
BUT NO WAY OUT
NO JOKING
NO HOPING
NO NOTHING
PINNED DOWN.

FAT GREASY SHRINKS
NOSEY BASTARDS
GOT NO REASON
FOR THE THINGS
THEY ASK YOU
KEEP YOU THERE
IN A HOLE
TILL YOU'RE READY
FOR JAIL AND DOLE
TAKE AWAY YOUR SOUL
PINNED DOWN.

WAKE UP AND YOUR HEART'S
NOT BEATING
TRY TO KILL YOURSELF
BUT THEY GOT YOU
BEATEN
YOU TRY TO TAKE IT
AWAY FROM THEM
ONCE, THEN TWICE
AND THEN AGAIN AND
AGAIN AND AGAIN AND
AGAIN AND AGAIN.
JUMP OUT OF THE WINDOW
SLASH YOUR WRISTS
ALL YOU REALLY WANTED
WAS TO SCREW AND GET PISSED.
AND THE SKY IS BLACK
BUT YOU CAN'T GO BACK
AND THE WAY AHEAD JUST LEADS TO
THE CHANDLER CLINIC.
AND THERE'S NOTHING THERE
EXCEPT MADNESS AND DESPAIR
PINNED DOWN.

DEHYDRATION
HUMILIATION
DEGRADATION
MIND CASTRATION
AND THE SKY IS BLACK
AND THE ONE NEXT TO YOU
KEEPS THINKING.
THEY'RE HAVING A HEART ATTACK.
PINNED DOWN.

DESOLATION
ON MEDICATION
NURSE NURSE NURSE
I CAN'T SLEEP
NURSE NURSE NURSE
CAN I HAVE MORE PLEASE
NURSE NURSE NURSE
NOW THEY GOT YOU
ON YOUR FUCKING KNEES
THAT'S WHERE THEY LIKE
YOU TO BE
ECT DID A JOB ON ME.
PINNED DOWN.

The Dunes

IT'S TRUE I WAS A DOCTOR'S SON
AND YET I GAZED IN WONDER
AS WE PERISHED FROM THE RAGING PLAGUE
THAT CAME WITH THE GREAT HUNGER
THAT CAME WITH THE GREAT HUNGER

I TRAVELLED TO THE WESTERN SHORE
SAW HUGE MOUNDS BUILT OF SAND THERE
FULL OF ROTTING BODIES OF SOULS
THAT DIED FROM THE GREAT HUNGER
THAT DIED FROM THE GREAT HUNGER

I SAW DEAD WOMEN IN THE DITCHES
WITH BABIES ONE OR YOUNGER

POISON BERRIES IN THEIR MOUTHS
TO TRY TO ESCAPE THE HUNGER
TO TRY TO ESCAPE THE HUNGER

BRITANNIA'S WHORES TOOK ALL OUR GRAIN
TO PUT BREAD ON THEIR TABLES
WHILE WALKING SKELETONS CRAWLED TO THE
BOATS
TO ESCAPE IF THEY WERE ABLE
TO ESCAPE IF THEY WERE ABLE.

I SAW THEM SCURRYING ON THE BOATS
PANICKING AND FRANTIC
YET MOST OF THEM THEY PERISHED STILL
TRYING TO CROSS THE BROAD ATLANTIC
TRYING TO CROSS THE BROAD ATLANTIC.

Amber Marks was born in London in 1977. In 1984 her family moved to Palma de Mallorca, Spain. In 1996 Amber returned to London and currently resides there.

Tell Me

'Cause I just can't believe you would lose us,
Over nothing really at all,
Unless we're not what you prayed for,
And it wasn't you in my dreams,
If you weren't there with the mushrooms, and the river and
the morning and the trees . . .
....

Am I not what you dreamt of?
Are we not what you prayed for?
Have we changed very much?
Are we not who you would have raised?
Do we drag on your conscience,
Like you dragged on ours?
Is it all done and over?
Have you come home and left?
Should we stop our praying?
Is there no one left to cry for?
Was our family ruined
A long time ago?

Was it foolish not to think so?
Was it wrong to deem it a matter of time?
It was a matter of time,
It was a matter of time

Has the clock stopped running?
Should we turn our eyes away?
Or is someone just pretending
And it will all be fine one day?
'Cause I love that day so dearly,
I've been waiting all the time.
And we don't mind waiting,
If you promise there is still time.

Did it come and I not notice,
Did I not see you when you came
Did you not see me waiting
In the corner by the tree,
Did I miss you walking?
Could you have been walking with me?
Did I forget to hold your hand?
Did you give it to me?

Or were you disillusioned when you saw me,
Did you think it best not to disturb,
Did I look as if I was busy?
Did you not see the tears?

Have you forgotten the laughter,
Are we just blood and tears?
Don't you know you're sought after?
Can't you come over here?

Will you read this and think little,
Add it up in your mind,
With some other considerations,
Some other tricks on your mind?

Is it all just a sad tale,
That I could tell as a joke?
Or is it all just a nightmare,
Not for ordinary folk.

Mummy

Home was in your arms.
I loved being your little girl,
The one you kept safe
And warm.

How I ached for those cuddles.
That day in the visiting room,
When they were pulling us apart,
I honestly thought they were tearing out my heart.

I used to creep into your wardrobe,
Lie down on your clothes.
The smell of you brought me to tears
But the feel of them soon dried them.

Again I came to see you.
This time you were further away.
A bright pink headband crowned your hair.
Greens and purples were painted on your face.
You sat smiling at me,
Like a helpless Baby Jane,
Waiting for my praise,
Silently smiling for my support,

When I so desperately needed yours.

Home
And I begged for things to be the same.
But you were a stranger
And though I remembered
How I'd ached to hold you,
Now you were here
I hardly went near.
The little girl continued aching,
But the teenager had no arms.

The days you used to hold me,
Home was in your arms.

They shattered the picture,
Smashed it into fragments,
Tiny bits and pieces laughing in my mind
Tiny bits and pieces that I will never find.

The child has lost her arms
And the woman has lost her heart,
Neither has a home,
Since they ripped her home apart.

Formed around the nucleus of singer and lyricist **Aidan Moffat** and guitarist Malcolm Middleton in 1995, Arab Strap are true troubadours telling the tale as they live it. Aidan and Malcolm were arrested together and between them they have created some of the most stark and observant music of the 90s. They have released as singles 'The First Big Weekend'; 'The Clearing', 'The Girls of Summer' EP 'Holiday Girl' (a reworking of David Holmes 'Don't Die Just Yet'), 'Here We Go'/'Trippy', and the albums *The Week Never Starts Round Here*, *Philophobia* and *Mad for Sadness*. They hail from Falkirk.

I'm Not Bitter

i tried to be clever and call your bluff,
you tried to punch me and packed up my stuff.
i pretended for ages i'd stopped eating meat,
you said i can fucking sleep in the street.
when you took my hand i'd fill up with pride,
but we stayed in a lot and now you're just wide.
and now that i'm sober and stopped fucking weeping,
i can't say there's much that you gave me worth keeping.

Cunts

We like to fuck and shag, we're not into making love
but i hope that she'd admit that we've done all of the above.
I've got a cock or sometimes willy, i'm referred to as her bird,
and she's usually got a fanny, rarely any other word,
though you might've heard a pie once, or a bum-not-back-but-
    front,
or maybe the odd snatch, but never once a cunt.
She only uses that word when it's Scottish for amigo,
or to punctuate a sentence when deflating my wee ego.

Henry Normal is one of the most original talents to emerge on the comedy circuit in recent years. He is popular both as a performance poet and as a stand-up alternative comic. He has performed in every kind of venue, from theatres to prisons and libraries, in pop concerts and on numerous radio and television programmes. He has appeared in cities throughout the world, from New York to Helsinki, as well as several times on the Edinburgh Fringe.

He was the originator, star and co-writer of Channel Four's *Packet of Three*. He co-writes Paul Calf with Steve Coogan and has been a scriptwriter for a number of other comedy programmes. *Nude Modelling for the Afterlife* (Bloodaxe Books, 1993) is his book of poetry.

Time passed unnoticed until she took the clock

Slumped on your chair like dead weight at an orgy
coughing like an S-reg Fiat
though you've lit up a thousand churches in prayer
you know
     she's not coming back

Overfat on time, you say 'age doesn't matter' then you lie
    about your own
if you live to be 100 you'd still be afraid of dying too
    young
Switching off the bedside lamp shadows crowd the void
but the patterns on the wallpaper don't scare you any more
it's the blank spaces now that threaten
Nothing, not even love, survives within a vacuum

Fast approaching your love-by-date
you count the days left unkissed
Age
   has become just another stick to beat yourself with
Where once your passion was an elevator between Heaven
   and Hell
Where once you believed love dripped from between her
   legs
There in the absence of children
sex grew tired on easy living, becoming a parasite on the
   back of routine and all the words your chose so carefully
blew like so much litter
Conversations became quieter
and as scarce as a spaghetti western
Laughter became a missing person
until you couldn't remember kissing her face when you last
   made love
and her lips became just hooks to hang your heart upon
and though you look for that face from the window of
   every train
the photo in your pocket is now starting to fade
and though you curse the new diary with each year that
   arrives
you never noticed the clock on the wall until it kissed you
   goodbye
you never noticed the clock on the wall until it kissed you
   goodbye

Whether satirising the pretensions of ageing rock stars, recounting the fallout of collapsing relationships or describing the poignancy of fatherhood, **Nigel Planer** revealed a sure poetic touch in his first collection of poems called *Unlike The Buddha* (Jackson's Arm, 1997).
Having originally made his mark as the hippy Neil in *The Young Ones*, Nigel Planer went on to establish himself as an accomplished actor in theatre, film and TV. *The Right Man* (Arrow, 1999) is his first novel.

Ex-Hippies

These moisturised forty-nine year olds
with silk shirts and linen suits
and wild, well-documented pasts,
in which they fucked famous girls
while the rest of us wanked,
who claimed, when young, to have alternative goals,
who talked of tokes, now take their toots,
and, hanging up their revolutionary guitars at last,
quaff champagne at a reunion gig and spout their recycled
   pearls
of wisdom and, middle-aged, expect to be thanked

for what they did for the coming New Age,
now living on residuals from their halcyon days
(the sixties, of course, when you could do what you liked),
are fatter now than when Aquarius dawned,
and have flown in from LA their favourite vegetarian chef
and shoved a fading minor pop-star on stage.
In colour supplement eulogies they
omit to tell us of the lives they wrecked,
the groupies and chicks, children that they spawned,
tried out new lifestyles on, then left.

Clare Pollard survived a Bolton Comprehensive and an out-of-school education at the town's indie nightclub to play the electric guitar with unrivalled incompetence, as well as to study English at Cambridge. Her poems have already appeared in many magazines. She read a poem in the toilets at the Ritzy for a recent BBC Talent 2000 documentary, and was a *Poetry Review* New Poet of '96.

A Friday Night at the end of a Millennium

On the first of January
in the year 2000
I will be twenty-one.
Yes, I am a woman

of the next millennium;
star on the clean black.
Our hope for the future.
but I don't give a fuck

as I check my pocket:
purse, lipstick, rape alarm;
and I'm out for the night in a town
where only rain glitters.

Air slits up my wrists
as I head for the pub.
Tottering on thin heels,
a cripple.

We get a seat by the TV screen.
Neck squirming-sour vodka and tonics;
pose with Budweiser bottles.
Soon we are watching *Casualty* with no sound on.

I get cheese and onion crisps.
We gossip to convince our veins
they are not stagnant with boredom.
The room looks like our lounge;

oak beams and a mock-Turkish carpet.
It is full of men who look as though they'd
play dominoes given half a chance.
one winks at me –

And I sneer the sneer of the young and slim.
He could cut his fist on me.
The week's blunt misery
dissolves with the salt off the peanuts.

My mate's called Kerry
and she's game for anything.
Slept with three Ouzo-slick Greeks
on holiday this summer –

sticky one-night stands,
and she's not ashamed.
No, she's proud as can be,
flashing blurred pictures

of her topless. Him fumbling
in his pocket for a spare condom.
At ten we head for the club.
It's symbolically underground.

: Clare Pollard

I order a pint for a pound,
sit on a cracked back chair and begin
to get intoxicated. My ex is here
selling cannabis to pre-pubescent

girls with ultra-bras,
pierced noses, plum hair
and nicotine-gilded fingers.
He is beautiful,

an angel in some lights.
He laughs at everyone,
and is too clever for this world;
fingers greasy with lightly salted puppy fat.

He sweats; snorts vodka
until his nose bleeds prettily.
Laughs some more, then
makes a pass at me on the stairs.

Shit, he is beautiful,
but he only wants me
to prove he gets what he wants –
so I push him away.

The only boy I ever liked to kiss.
It makes me sad but proud.
I have won.
I will learn to live without

his static lips,
the warm dark sparks
that danced softly off his
fingers down my spine.

Dizzy with the punch of winning, I dance.
Jump up and down
like I'm tied to this rotten ceiling with elastic.
I swing my hips,

and lick my lips –
they are dry with cider,
flavoured with salt
and hard-jawed smiles.

I enjoy dancing.
There is a kind of freedom in it,
energy pounding out
of my hunched-up joints.

From the floor I watch
a boy who told me he thinks
I am very attractive –
but he's sleeping with her now.

The big commitment –
get them in bed
and they're caged. Hooked.
Can't wriggle free.

His hair is chilli-red,
his eyes fish scales,
his smile a small boy's.
I used to get giddy when I saw him –

Now I just feel weighted.
Tired. My bones will shatter
like peanut brittle or barley sugar
or some other crap sweet.

Another pint, and they charge
me two pounds this time –
they must have seen me staggering,
but I'm too drunk to care.

Alcohol goes straight through me.
The girls' loos are full
of lads smoking joints,
so I have to piss quietly,

hovering over the bowl
as though I'm a hummingbird
in order to avoid diseases.
Stale urine.

Someone's bloody tampon goads me redly.
I read the sign on the toilet door,
it says: 'AVOID UNWANTED
PREGNANCY – USE A TELEPHONE.'

Oh, that used to make us laugh
when this bitter-dark club seemed new;
when this tongue-moist air
didn't catch in my throat

like a wishbone. I always wish
for something utterly impossible:
lager that hasn't been watered down,
a star, him.

The poor wish fairies –
I am expecting miracles!
It isn't fair on them.
This bad luck is my own responsibility.

It is my own fault,
I take all the blame.
I vow to aim lower and stop thinking
I'm the fucking second coming,

then pull up my silk copping-knickers.
Stumble out, eyes greyed
by a gauze of yeast.
Mirror, mirror on the wall,

says I'm the biggest dog of all.
My flaws glow vivid.
nuclear white light strips my skin off
and leaves the true-me clean.

A regular ugly sister.
Leaves me like a plucked turkey;
face withered and swollen with heat,
lips just a parched outline.

My arms are gorilla hairy in the brightness.
My lip is bald, because I scorched off the hair
before I came out,
with a cream that claimed to be rose

but stank of shit.
My armpits are stubbly jutting caves.
I put deodorant on after shaving
and they stung as though wasps

had built nests in the coves
of dark, moist calcium.
I have a good itch of my bikini line,
readjust my hair – it's sucked sweet sticky.

One lad is trying on his girlfriend's eyeshadow.
Having a good laugh.
It makes me sick-green
to see them crackling with happiness;

to see their reflections —
quivering jelly-fish with hysterics.
He suits it—it is glossy purple,
a pair of artfully blackened eyes.

I watch my nails as I wash my hands.
See I've chipped the *Madly Midnight* polish,
and it sounded so exciting too!
I try to say 'Hi' to someone on the stairs,

only to find my pickled tongue snow-numb.
I cannot speak, mind bleak
as a figureless, hospital-white
winter horizon.

Sitting by the slot machine
that says *Win! Win! Win!*
in the hope its optimism
might rub off,

I listen to
I'm Only Happy When It Rains.
Lose me in empty Diamond White bottles.
Watch others dance,

limbs flying as though
they are epileptic.
All want to pull
but many are too scared.

(What if something falls off?)
Stickily laughing,
I worry about smeared make-up, taxi fares,
my omnipresent virginity — the usual.

Then the inevitable accident —
sweet, sweet cider down
my new blue dress.
I drip like an icicle —

force a smile when a man
in skin-tight army pants
offers to lick it all off
of me for free.

Looking down, I notice
my thighs are exposed.
Our skirts get shorter every week.
My knickers playing hide and seek!

A boy approaches, he is unremarkable,
but at least I feel no nausea.
I may go with him to enhance
my pitiful total of boys kissed so far.

Only I've done that before —
and it leaves me soiled.
The sickening unfamiliarity
of strange tongues;

moist muscle choking you.
A heaving of flesh
with a bruised bud texture
that tastes of vinegar

or, worse, tea-time hot pot.
Dead meat or apples
that have browned for months.
And it either chokes you –

suffocates as though you've
swallowed an Asda bag;
or they're gentle and sloppy –
slobbering dog-like

over your chin, your neck,
your upper lip.
Giving you a wet moustache.
Snail slime slippery

and filling your throat
with its unknown glue-juice
until you want to hide
slug pellets behind your lower teeth.

If you're lucky they'll just
move their tongue in circles –
as though they are drawing
balloons or coins with it.

The monotony dulls your senses
and loosens your jaw.
You want to eat him –
not through lust but

for the thrill of his head in your gullet.
Blood spurting brightly from his warm neck vein,
and you'd swallow it like medicine.
At least then it would be over.

Their stubble grazes your chin,
until it feels as your knees did
when you fell on stony ground as a child.
And if you open your eyes – ugh!

Lids curtain-closed with bliss
as though they're on a train to Paradise,
when you're feeling queasy
and are itching to get free.

Their indignity is distasteful,
their knowledge of your precious mouth.
You want to slap them.
Burn all official records of their being.

Their pleasure and shut-eyed fun is a sick joke –
they think you like them!
It is at times like that
I realise what an ugly word 'snogging' is.

Sometimes, I find myself
Looking around – that's the killer.
Suddenly, you care what everyone thinks;
blush rare-beef pink.

Roast hotly with the realisation
he is not cool, or handsome,
and his character is dubious –
this boy who has his

salivary glands pumping for you.
Who you are sharing spit with.
And you cringe, wince,
try to arrange your hair differently

so nobody will recognise you.
You and this grotesque,
macabre, bladdered freak.
The one with his hands

on your thighs, your back,
the nape of your neck.
He even tries to cop a good
feel up your top –

the nerve of him to think
you are in his league.
On his level.
Not too special to touch.

Anyway, I decide not to go with him.
Laugh for a while as a blond, gay Goliath
licks a hard stripe down
my homophobic male mate's cheek.

My ex reappears,
now vitriolic and revenge-bent;
picks on my sparkly shoes,
and the way I've mislaid my purse.

Flirts violently with
other lager blondes
before my same stale face,
trying to make me cry boozily,

how little he knows me!
I never break,
but am strong as cartilage.
Look, my legs flex as though made of it.

Lights flutter like dying butterflies
in the hot whisky crush.
I am no one, smudged.
A happy blur.

'Are you okay?' someone asks,
and I nod cow-like.
Look at my watch
but see no time, no movement.

Kerry's in the corner
fumbling jumpily with a lad,
legs clenched tightly round him.
People stare a bit, giggling,

then give her a round of applause
when she comes up for air.
She reddens, but not much,
for she loves attention.

Adores a starring role.
Oh, she is a wild-child!
I look shocked, for
it pays to humour her.

See, even drunk I am condescending!
People stomp on my feet.
Rip my tights with careless,
skeletal fingers.

They are trying to destroy me!
I thumb the hole
until it gapes.
A moon made of

lightly downed thigh flesh.
The gold of the hairs shimmers.
Magic dust. Then they
stand erect like little warriors,

and I feel like a hermaphrodite,
and cover it guiltily
as though it is a ripped hymen.
It is cold in here.

So cold I would gasp,
had I the will power
or the energy.
A consuming coldness.

I am a dead foetus
dunked in a lab-jar of ice water.
Exposed and raw,
and I can't feel my pulse,

just the throbbing
of a headache coming on.
Oh, it hurts –
and they've started playing

that terrible Prodigy song.
You know, the one that goes
I've got the remedy, but
only makes me long for Paracetamol.

My stomach churns –
that last pint tipped me over.
My mouth is dry
as a burnt moth.

I perch on the radiator.
Watch my hand clenching
and opening in the darkness.
A sea anemone.

I watch all the people.
The ones who will
dance into the glorious
sunrise with me.

The ones who will kick-start
a new, shining era.
The leaders of men
who will gush like fresh blood

into the next century.
Sacrificial lambs.
The whitest of white;
the brightest flames.

They are joking about blow jobs.
They are inventing nasty
names for one another –
like Trout Eyes.

They are spilling Newcastle Brown
down their Adidas three-stripe tops
and beckoning people
who scare them in broad daylight.

Adjusting spiked hair
and gold hooped eyebrows
in the mirrors of dull
alcoholic lemonade bottles.

And kissing.
Fingering each other's writhing maggot bodies
as though they were cut-glass
or braille or made of flowers.

They are glugging down doubles
with competitive grins.
Shimmying round the shattered shards
of smashed pint mugs

that blossom. An ice web.
They are vomiting a cocktail
of bitter and bile
on the threadbare stairs.

So many people and they all
only want to be loved.
Funny isn't it?
How all could love fiercely

if they only got the chance,
But they won't. It's sad.
Like spilt lager.
Like the taxi ride home.

Martin Preston has been writing poetry and short stories
and performing extensively for the last ten years, mainly in Brighton but also
in London, Bristol and Bath.

Martin has performed with Herbert Hunke, Carolyn Cassady, Jake Black
(Alabama 3), David Allen (Gong) and Will Self. He was in the runners-up
team at the UK Poetry Slam – where he scored a perfect 10 (from John
Cooper Clark) and won the South East Arts Performance Poetry Bursary
Award in 1997.

Shedding Skin

When death opened her deep red mouth
I walked right in
and kept on walking
when I could barely crawl no more
I kept on walking
past the hermaphrodite whores
of the world
too ugly to look at
I listened to the despair of children
waiting to be born
I locked horns
with my deepest
maddest
darkest self
and just kept right on walking
into pit black self
and there I witnessed my own death
and saw the sorry mess I created
as I lay there

at the bottom of the sea
lost in deadly still darkness
a pin hole of light
pierced the womb
like a star being born
and I cried
as the moon pulled me up
on a silver shaft of light
and sure enough
I was reborn
another life
within this lifetime
on one condition
I acknowledge the death
of my previous self.

I am telling you this
cos I love you.

Poet, playwright and musician, **James Raiher** grew up in
London and studied sociology and philosophy at Royal Holloway College.
Fascinated by language and performance, he has worked in television,
publishing and theatre. He has travelled widely and once almost went to Las
Vegas.

I Am Not An Alcoholic

I am not an alcoholic
because vodka always plays second fiddle to the delicate art
  of conversation
although I can't be bothered to stand up

I am not an alcoholic
because I often drink coffee without whisky
and I have no opinions

but I have my standards, eh?
which all but disappeared a while ago
when things were good
the connection is far from obvious to me
but in this context
nothing is clearer

I'll try anything once
become obsessed, then give it up completely and never
  look back
maybe I just don't give a shit
but by the looks of things neither do you

all that's important is under my mattress
although it's on the floor
people, politics and all that crap
but at least they're comfortable
and not crushed by the weight of flashing lights and imbeciles
at the gym all day quite near the river
because context isn't just what but who you are
I am not an alcoholic because that's no cure for
limitless overdrive anti-gravity Nike shellsuits

let's paint road lines the colours of the political parties
yellow, red but blue?
no that wouldn't do
so we're all floating voters, or at least we're all floating
and there's a two hour maximum stay
but I know all of this is mixed up
woods and trees are all the same to me

anyway it's no wonder I'm broke
switch receipts are made of recycled paper
any old drainage system will do
go for a swim in a cleansing station
puddles don't do the trick, no joke
poker-faced clever-dicks all of you

I am not an alcoholic because I saw
Leaving Las Vegas and Nicholas Cage was just wonderful
so now I suppose he's a millionaire
which means all the drink he wants, eh?
but I don't resent that
and I hope he wasn't getting any ideas there
you know, method acting and that

and I know an all-night liquor store
within two miles from . . . time gentlemen please

days get incrementally worse
until . . .
gradually worse
until . . .
progressively worse
until . . .

come back to me
I am not an alcoholic
because neither are you
you always said we had a lot in common
now drink your words
I only drink for fun
I like having fun
and so do you

benefits, benefits, benefits
all I ever hear
small print gives me a headache
it's just an admission of a crap situation
benefits means: in this world
something bearable
like chip fat and chips
roadworks and roads
love and sex

I am not an alcoholic
I rely on reality
and I have never distilled anything myself, but confusion

Paul Reekie

Paul Reekie was born in the early sixties between the *Lady Chatterley's Lover* trial and the Beatles' first LP. He was brought up in the paper-making town of Leslie, mostly near the pen factory, and has been resident in Leith for the last twenty years. He once claimed Adam Smith and Michael Scott of Balwearie as ancestors, but has since realised that a man who goes on about his illustrious ancestors is like a potato – in that the greater part of him lies under ground.

His verses have appeared in such publications as *Parabola, Infinity, Compendium Review, Curtains* (Maidstone) and the *Glasgow Herald*. He wrote an unwittingly libellous novella which appeared in the *Children of Albion Rovers* anthology (Rebel Inc.) and gave his first reading of poetical work at the David Hume Tower, Edinburgh, in 1982. Since then he has read in most major European countries and beyond, from the Goethe Institute, Cairo, to the Co-Existence Bagel Shop, San Francisco.

He is currently writing an historical novel with the working title *The Scottish Patient*.

Irish Lassies Shag Like Fuck

(For Linton Kwesi Johnson who told me slackness was nothing new)

It's said God gave us memory so that
We should have roses in December
Someone told me the first story is
Two people go up a hill and find a snake   (. . . yess . . .)
But we think it's *Irish lassies shag like fuck*.

Remember you were the blue mountain flower
Making love alfresco – for those that know
Is the very very first go

(Unless of course you come from Glasgow
Where it is standing up in a close)
At leisure; Arty but not crafty fancy fuckings.

                          (. . . E. Gill . . .)

Remember you were the blue mountain flower
We had come from the High Inn
Making our way to the West Law
Then all the outline of her person
contained the land.
Hazel level on the hot grass.
Dear Friend, never seen what was behind Hazel's knickers
   so . . .
Brightly lit.   (Aye freckles)

Remember you were the blue mountain flower.
You were that day.
Many hundreds of years before the revolution
Old Geoff knew a song
Hail, hail the first of May
Outdoor fucking begins today.

Victim Of A Miracle

(Dedicated with gratitude to the firemen of Edinburgh who,
when a job is on are the opposite of hesitation, which is to say
they don't fanny about. God bless you boys)

I am reminded of the Guthrie St disaster
By the words of a party-hunting bore
'Why are they *always* on the top floor?'
Then BANG it's falling rubble and plaster

Jason lived on Guthrie St, the flat at the top
In a gas explosion if you don't want to be dead
You'd best be flexible, drunk and stoned in bed
Thus he survived the ninety foot drop

Awake and o.k. — a little bruising at the knees
Some firemen gathered round in the hospital
The nurses all agreed there'd been a miracle
The firemen handed Jason his front door keys

He'd had a new violin hanging on his wall
The fireman rescued it from the fallen rock
Playable, intact but for a scratch on the headstock
Jason giggled, remembering nothing of his fall

Jason's flatmate heard a vague noise that night
Keith paced drunkenly towards Jason's bedroom
Opening the door to say the least he took a fright

As there was nothing but fresh air, a tiny ridge
Way below he saw a rising cloud of brick dust
Above the night sky and George the IVth bridge

One more step and he goes all the way down
But he backs off, leaving by the front door
Keith knows for sure he won't sleep any more
Through debris and the Cowgate he heads for town

Heights and bridges are somehow on his mind
So he walks on towards the river Forth
Neither feeling the distance nor the cold wind of the north
Kelth reaches the road bridge with a purpose ill-defined

Doubling back on himself, wearying of the view
He plods all around town with crazy eyes
Simply not caring if he lives or if he dies
Wouldn't merit the attention of me or you

To an old lady, two days later at Leith docks
He said, 'I don't know who I am, I'm gone
And why have I got my pyjama trousers on?'
She puzzles, finds her purse and then a phone box . . .

Jason found himself another flat within a week
But Keith's been on counselling now a long time
Doesn't sleep, takes fits, will rarely speak

Won't say how he must hate his new nick-name
Unbelievably cruel bastards now call him Eppy
He witnessed a miracle but he'll never be the same.

Roger Robinson is a graduate of the infamous 'Speakers Corna' poetry jams (Brixton Art Gallery) and former member of the now disbanded Urban Poets Society and Chocolate Art. He has performed in such venues as the Institute of Contemporary Art, Barbican Centre, Institute of International Visual Arts and Royal Festival Hall, as well as in Germany, Holland, Canada and America.

He has been instrumental In programming poetry happenings and has facilitated workshops and lectures on poetry around London. He is presently the programmer for Apples & Snakes performance poetry agency, and was chosen in 1998 as one of thirty poets for the National Portrait Gallery's New Generation Poets Collection.

He was featured on the *Chocolate Art* EP on Earth Connection Records, Salvage Record's *Kinetic Sound System* EP and on the new album by Flytronix on Moving Shadow Records, as well as on Bammer Projects album and on the new Juryman album for K7 records. He has also been the opening act with his poetry for De la Soul, Run DMC and Attica Blues.

Lamentation for Stephen
(for murdered Stephen Lawrence)

I REMEMBER THE NIGHT WE HEARD
OUR FACES BECAME CREASED AND CREVICED AS
    EARTHQUAKES
EXPRESSIONS TIGHTENED LIKE TUG-OF-WAR
    ROPES.
EVEN THE CLOUDS IN THE NIGHT AIR WERE
    SYMPATHETIC,
ROLLING LIKE MILK IN BLACK TEA,
OR BILLOWING LIKE BLOOD IN WATER,
DEPENDING ON YOUR POINT OF VIEW.

WE WERE THE ONES WALKING DEAD IN ALL BUT
   NAME
WITH YAWNING, YELPING, VOICES OF ANGERED
   PASSION
ECHOING LAMENTATIONS WITH NO ANSWERS,
BUT FOR MUTED THUNDER WITH A RASPING
   EDGE.

YOU, THE VIBRANT MAN BOY
YOUR LIFE CLEAVED CUT CARVED AWAY LIKE FAT
   FROM MEAT
LOOKING FORWARD TO GIRLFRIEND,
   GRADUATION AND GOOD TIMES,
LISTENING TO HIP-HOP AT THE BUS STOP ON
   YOUR HEADPHONES
IT'S TINNY DRUM RINGING IN YOUR EARS
THE LAST SOUND YOU'D HEAR AS YOU
   STRUGGLED TO ESCAPE
SLEEPS VIVID WIRE,
PAST THE DRAWN CURTAIN OF YOUR EYELIDS.

AND I USED TO BELIEVE IN PEACE AND JUSTICE
AND LOVE AND KARMA AND HOPE,
BUT I GUESS THERE AIN'T NO LOVE AND PEACE
   AND KARMA
AND HOPE FOR BLACK BOYS GAGGING
IN A POOL OF BLOOD AT THE BUS STOP
WITH HIP-HOP IN THEIR HEADPHONES.

THERE'S A DARKER SIDE TO THIS WRECK,
THE SIDE THAT MAKES A MOTHER WEEP MILKY
   TEARS,

LIKE A RUBBER TREE WEEPS SAP,
THE SIDE THAT MAKES A FATHER BURY HIS FACE
   IN HIS HANDS.

I HEARD YOU WERE BURIED FACING THE DAWN
   TO AVOID THE SMELL OF STORMS
FLOATING BLOOD AND EVIL SPIRITS.
STEPHEN, I SHALL GRAB LOOSE SOIL FROM YOUR
   GRAVE IN MY CLAWED FIST
AND POINT LIGHTED CANDLES TO THE SKY
AND SMILE IN THIS SERVICE ATTENDED BY MYSELF
   AND THE WIND.

Memoir

This sleeping woman
whose eyelids flutter moths
belying eyes like sun's eclipse,
whose lips quiver dreams on half smiles
as she sips breaths of rustling leaves,
her coffee-coloured curves lay
framed like some exquisite painting by the bed.

And outside sunlight blurs
the morning's edge
as sandalwood breezes
make morning birds bicker
I lean to kiss this dream
so as not to awaken her sleep
but to taste love's salty skin.

And for the rest of that morning
as our room dips below the sun,
that briny taste forces me to write
a crumpled confession about a woman
who placed her heart on my tongue
who rolled it around my lips and through my mind
who peppered inkblot kisses on my eyes
who smiled a shining mosaic of stars
that lit up the room
as we laughed our passion like gurgling water
as we poured into each other
again and again
on the precipice of dawn and definition
as froth crested waves
broke and reformed and broke.

And every year
a man tries to unwrinkle
a scribbled memoir
of a morning after a night
and remembers.

Jem Rolls has been running the poetry cabaret, Big Word, for the past five years. Having done eight hundred gigs, and promoted three hundred, he feels he is virtually unmatched in pushing forward the boundaries of performance poetry and in taking it to as wide a variety of spaces as possible.

I'd Rather Be Dead

neighbours twice a day?
i'd rather be dead
prince charles' sex life?
i'd rather be dead
i woke up this morning and i'd turned into a giant william hague?
i'd rather be dead
mechanical one-armed bandit handshake?
ten year smile like a synchronised swimmer?
the sun says?
VAT on fuel?
benefit axe?
penalty fare?
crinkly bottom?
hang'em birch'em lock'em up?
i'd rather be dead
sorry, we've only got john smiths
2 night buses home
no ticket inspector at the barrier, the time you buy a ticket
life in the bus lane?
over here's one i did earlier?
luxembourg deux points?
see that ashtray, that's you that is?
i do prefer the kind of jokes with humour in them?

the post-modernist always rings twice?
i'd rather be dead
tony blair's . . . significant . . . pauses
. . .

it took me two months to write that silence
paul johnson?
tv dinner?
job club?
police search?
capital gold?
north peckham estate?
british people in queues?
the page three girls get younger and sexier?
enjoy?
i'd rather be dead
monsieur, weev zees ferrero rocher you are really spoiling us
excellente, delicious
i'd rather be dead
make up to steal your time?
worries to worry about?
recipes to make you fat?
diets to make you thin again?
i'd rather be dead
only complete misery can make me happy
the light at the end of the tunnel
is for the sign which says, DEAD END
gridlocked brains
free-range serfdom, i repeat, free-range serfdom
self-love . . . pretentious? moi? . . .
i'm a passenger in me own head
i'd rather be dead
rules? britannia?

britannia waives the rules
and brits oo believe otherwise
can only ever lose
i'd rather be dead
the circle line I repeat the circle line
you call that thinking?
estate agents in suspended animation
lottery queues in voluntary taxation
the machines deserve to take over
at least we deserve to lose
the rspca castrated our cat without asking us
pavements are for wimps, so . . .
i'd rather be dead
birmingham i repeat birmingham
eyebrow deep up shit creek
a movie to titillate only the most pathetically, frustrate
baywatch boyzone blackleg
bint slut slag bitch
tequila slammers with tennants super for the mix?
queen camilla?
brink like a sick?
m25?
lady porter? lady archer? lord archer? mark thatcher?
fur coat? slug and lettuce? racist bastards?
brand new superstore?
what do you think of this colour?
no-no no-no-no-no no-no-no-no
i'd rather be dead
criminal justice bill?
flexible working?
i got mugged by a second-hand record-shop
that's the kind of guy i am?

oo you lookin at?
any kind of nationalism?
i'd rather be dead
magenta da halfwit?
the man from del monte says?
they should bring back el dorado?
they're not as good as they used to be?
it's the way you tell'em?
cor bleedin blinkin blimey
i'd rather be dead
the poetry society
irony blinkin' irony?
can neither mean what i say
nor say what i mean?
as jean baudrillard once said
i'd rather be dead
watching the grass grow?
death by sitcom?
can't see the dull for the dullness?
using words till they run out of meaning?
i'd rather be dead
help!
i'd rather be dead
stop, no more, thank you
i'd rather be dead

Gareth Sager was born in Edinburgh, moved to Bristol, moved to London. He has recorded twelve albums: *Y, For How Much Longer, We Are Time, God, I Am Cold, Attitude, Kill Me In The Morning, A Snog On The Rocks, Tales Of Ordinary Madness, Intoxicator, Unusual Lover, Weep Hippies Weep*.

He has also performed in hundreds of concerts with The Pop Group, Rip, Rig and Panic, Float Up CP, Head, Pregnant, and solo in Europe, Japan and the USA. He is currently working on a film and ice show extravaganza of 'The Seven Books Of The Great Path, According To The Late Lama Kazi Dawa-Sandup's English Rendering'.

My Stags And Hens Mobile Disco

No condition is permanent
That's what I saw written on the pavement
Pigmeat, Piano, Pigment . . . This man has a hairdresser's name!
Training us to flock . . .
Abiding his time in the waterfall
A knight between Death and the Devil
See me I ain't got the lingo
But time was always officer material
This caveman music woke me, it spoke to me
So I looked out of the window . . .
And there working the village hall
Was my stags and hens mobile disco
Now Heaven and Hell co-exist in my bliss station
A fine balancing act . . . 3 points to the other side
Let's weigh it up, soon come another turn in the tide
Till it's still . . . It's still . . .

Burton's 1st XV

You think I'm Richard Burton
Gone missing behind the royal curtain
With firewater breath and feeling so unblessed
Don't let your sleeping dogs lie
Listen to the nightmare children cry
There's nothing like an uninvited guest
To bring out the worst in the best
Well that's my opinion more or less

Thrilled to the gills,
We fired up the night
Watched the man, turn it on
Just like Christmas lights
He said 'What a pair of pins'.
'You're seeing double', 'No! they're twins'
Smitten by the grape once again my friend
Yeah we're seasick as a dog, down by Stoke Lodge
My weeping eyes can't save me from my past . . . alas

The Valley Boy felt the witch's blade
Trying to stay curious not afraid,
The purple-eyed Tailor
Spoke of his success and failure
'See his mam was saying no
while father urged have a go'
Rebellion never leads to love
He'd have swapped all his cash and fame
Just to have played in one great game,
So try again, Velvet Voice, how pain is your ally.

Chris Savage King is a writer and performer. She left school at sixteen to work, but later trained as a dancer and studied English. She has written for a range of publications from *Marxism Today* to *Harpers & Queen*. In 1996 she won the ICA Award for Writing for Performance and has since performed in a variety of venues. She is currently writing *Britart*, a book of cultural commentary, for Serpent's Tail. *Do What You Want*, her first novel, is published by Pulp Books.

Boy

There was a boy, 21
Soft baby skin, plump hard muscles
Who I used to see every now and again

Christ, you said, *that's not love darling* some kind of
    arrangement like *that*
That's not love darling
Have a bit of self respect
As you bombed down the stairs to the tube one night

Well yes it was a bit basic
That *arrangement*, as you put it
He had little English
I had less Spanish
He said 'I *luff* you *darling*' quite a lot
He said it very deliberately
Not the same way you did
Lionheart
I never learned the Spanish for 'I love you darling'
Actually

I'm not that foolish
I know what love is
I think

Were you jealous?
I mean – was that why you got off with the
pouting Portuguese girlie that night?
And told me all about it?
Trying to be objective
I offered my congratulations
You huffed and puffed
Yeah – but it's not as if it *meant anything*, did it?

After our affair was well and truly through
Once you were finally with someone who *meant something*
I got another earful
When I told you about a bit of distracted snogging and
    touching up
I'd done the previous evening
So innocent and silly it wouldn't offend the Pope

I'll tell you something though
The *luff* of the Latin beefcake caused me far less heartache
Than your subsequent version
Of the Real Thing
And less bliss too, of course

Red Hot Lust

Red hot lust has its own
demented momentum
It can find a home in anyone
It thrives quite a lot when there's no action
But thrives even more on a little

I'm not sure I ever felt as restless as that time
When you were there and not there
Not starting anything nor finishing it either
Dispensing your favours so occasionally
You don't think of anything else
The day after the last time
Whenever it was
I was so distracted I didn't know what to do with myself
Thanks a lot, I intended to read
But it wore off
Or at least affixed itself
To someone else
More generous
More out there
Who loved me
It always does

Red hot lust
Lust in the dust
Ashes to ashes
Dust to dust

Born on 21 September 1952 in Leith, Edinburgh, **Jock Scot** was one
of seven children and had a happy childhood until his father's death in 1967.
After a stint as a lumberjack, librarian and farm labourer he then embarked on
a career as a rock promoter and DJ at Tiffany's ballroom in Edinburgh whilst all
the time secretly writing poetry, a passion he'd had since childhood. Jock then
became involved with the punk scene of the late seventies, working for The
Clash, Ian Dury and the Blockheads, Blondie, Talking Heads and the B52s; and
after waking up in a broom cupboard after a particularly arduous tour he
decided to settle in London and start performing his poetry. In 1993 his book
Where Is My Heroine was published and it was around this time that he made
his first excursions onto vinyl and CD, culminating with his own album *My
Personal Culloden* which was released in May 1998. Jock was one of the first
performance poets to record for MTV. He also performs with Davy Henderson
and The Nectarine No. 9.

Thunder Over Kilburn

Although I won't be there with you this evening
To watch you as you strip and change for bed
Pull the covers back and then embrace me
As my shoulder makes a pillow for your head.

In my thoughts I will be there, as you move closer
In my thoughts, I am beside you and no other.
And when I dream, I'll dream of when,
I last kissed your eyes and then,
Changed position slightly,
As you parted my thighs I lifted your nightie.
We snogged, and you drew near,
You whispered in my ear
'What have we got here?'

But it's raining hard tonight here,
Up in Kilburn.
The drunken men cannot find their way home.
They stagger and then fall down in the gutter,
Singing sad laments of love gone wrong.
Thank God! That it will soon be tomorrow
And I'm not lying, soaked-out, in the street
I'll call you when I wake up baby,
If, I can just get off to sleep.

R.N.L.I.

Like a lifeboat you came to my rescue.
Through storm-tossed seas of never-could-be,
With me drowning in their midst,
Standing on my own at the bar
Pathetically, hopelessly pissed.
Grace Darling could not have done better,
The water could not have been wetter.
'Ship ahoy! Ship ahoy!' that's the sailor's cry.
My eyes were wet and my throat was dry,
As you hove-to in the crowded bar.
The fog it was lifted and so was my jar.
'Who stole my fuckin' pint!'

Nectarine No. 9

Girls may come and girls may go
And you'd just come along,
To hear the band up on the stage
Wrestle with their new songs
Which they said were from the forthcoming album
I think it was called 'Saint Jack'.
Or something equally meaningful
Me, I was standing at the back.

Needing time to think, I bought you a drink
But you were already staring at the singer,
Davy fuckin' Henderson,
Dressed-up like a dug's dinner.
He flicked the fringe out of his eyes
And slowly ground his hips,
You drank the drink I'd bought for you
And then you licked your lips.

The maverick popsters' guitars jangled
As they hopped around the stage,
Their flex was getting all tangled
As I strove to contain my rage.
I couldn't take any more of it
My opium-suppositries were kickin'–in
And I felt like kickin'
Henderson's fuckin' heid in
But I wouldn't know where to begin,
Being completely non-violent,
So I just swallowed the rest of my mother's Valium
And went very, very quiet.

Brinsley Sheridan was born in 1950 in Monaghan, Ireland and is married with two children and has been living in Dulwich for the last twenty-five years. He sells used cars for a living.

He has always been a prolific writer and his first job was writing a TV column in Ireland. He has performed in the UK and in the US at the Austin Poetry Festival (for two years running) and many times on radio. He has also performed his poetry on MTV World-wide for 15 seconds!

He hosts music and poetry evenings at Bunjies and the Twelve Bar Club.

BMW

I'm a brand new BMW, my wheels are bright and shining
And I've just been parked by Mark outside the restaurant
　　where he's dining.
He's a senior account executive with Tackie Snitch and
　　Borrow
He handles soaps & toiletries and tampons that cure
　　sorrow.
He sells us dreams on little screens that make life seem so
　　simple
Where every home's a germ-free zone and every cheek is
　　dimpled.
His job is to convince us that what we have is what we are
And as he just bought me today – that makes him a
　　German car.

I'm a year old BMW, my wheels are bright and gleaming
And I've just been parked by Margaret at her five bed det.
　　in Ealing

Now Bill bought me so that Margaret could get the
  shopping and the kids from school
He also hopes I'll cheer her up a bit, as he's away a lot.
  Bill's a fool!
Mark's tampons didn't cheer her up nor did his toiletries
  or soap
Which is why Mark got made redundant and how I became
  Bill's hope.
Now I can cruise the autobahns at a hundred miles an hour
I was not designed to replace Love in marriages turned
  sour.

I'm a third-hand BMW, my wheels are clean and tidy
And I now belong to Jackie, hairdresser in the city,
  Monday to Friday.
She likes her weekends free you see to get out and have a
  laugh
And I'm good for that; reliable and I still add a touch of
  class.
But one day she'll get rid of me when it's time for home
  and kids
Right now, she says; 'Life's too short!' Besides! She's not
  yet met 'his nibs'.
Margaret has, by the way, his name's Kevin, he has a
  window round in Ealing
He tells her she's the greatest thing since sliced bread —
  she's beginning to believe him!

I'm a fourth-hand BMW; I've just been de-chromed and
  fitted
With a plastic colour-coded body-kit and a sound system
  that's wicked!

I cruise around Notting Hill all day – They call my man
King Cole

He got the grains that steal your brains – The dole queue
stole his soul.

Respect! He cries and spins my wheels. Respect! My engine
screams.

Respect me don't reject me like you did my childhood
dreams

Respect me brother, this car's a mother! Now I've got
dreams to sell!

Jackie's right! Life's short! So have a snort! A day's too
long in hell.

I'm a burned-out BMW, on a road in Parsons Green.

The king is dead; they cracked his head, for stealing his
own dreams.

But as I lie dying, hot metal sighing, cooling in the
midnight air

I rejoice that I'm a car and not on a par with you
intelligent beings out there

For I've had a little taste and seen a lot of waste of this
much praised human mind

Yet I shouldn't complain cause if you ever got sane you
might de-invent my kind

But let's not be sad it wasn't all bad. I was up, I was
down; rarely bored.

Life could have been worse; I might have been cursed; to
have lived and died – a Ford!

Hank Starrs is lyricist and singer with the band Animals That Swim. 'Bed Island' comes from the album *I Was The King, I Really Was The King* released on Elemental Records.
He has written a couple of plays that have been performed in both London and Glasgow and he is currently working on a screenplay, *Pablo and Casagemas*. Animals That Swim will be releasing a new album later this year.

Bed Island

One particular party
the bedroom was full of books
there was hundreds of them
red hardbacks
stacked up flat
all around the walls
in some places
as high as my shoulder.

I was jealous
why wasn't I that clever?
I wanted them all
sat in the centre of the huge bed
there I was
shitfaced on bed island.

Later
pinning some girl to the wall
with a gibberish rant
about Orson Welles.

Her half pint Spanish friend
screaming at me
why are you wearing that crucifix
around your neck?
you are not religious!

I told her I stole it from a drunken priest
after giving him a good thrashing
in a carpark.

For years afterwards
I tried to acquire book piles of my own
it never worked out

I got robbed
sold them for food
gave them away.

Finally I lost the urge
it really was a relief
all I've got now is a roadmap
and the tiger who came to tea.

Paul Stewart was born in Somerset in 1956 and brought up in Bristol. After gaining an MA in Theatre Studies at the University of North London, he now works as an independent researcher for writers, authors, journalists and historians. His poetry has appeared in many magazines. His hobbies include western horsemanship and he was fortunate enough to be trained by leading charros in Mexico; and when he's not riding in the Sierra Madre he can be found riding on Walthamstow Marshes in East London wearing his chaps.

I Love London

I love London
they said
looking at the sights
as they leaned against a lean-to
where a man spends his nights.

I love London
was their only refrain
as a youngster
lay sleeping
in a stationary train

So I said
I saw 'the fox'
down by Tower Bridge
said, I saw him rummaging
around refuse
and an old dumped fridge

And in the bins
at the back of supermarkets
you may find some Mother's Pride
but it's not just his pride he's lost
his mates just starved and died

Police find the bodies
on cold winter nights
dead from exposure
under bright city lights

And I love London
they said
looking at the sights
walking past shop doorways
someone's home
on homeless nights

I love London
was their only refrain
but care in the community
is face down in the drain

and down by the riverside
drivers in warm cars
driving
alongside
the boat
moving slowly
up the flowing river,
small cars
crawling up the Embankment

a splash of white snow
on a cardboard home
that shifts
shivers
and coughs
as cars hiss by
in this old city
this cold city
of cold hearts.

How High Can A Kestrel Fly?

How high can a kestrel fly?
Hovering over its nest
on high-rise IBM
It rises high over Gunnersbury trains
That link North London
Where, now it rains,
Or west to Kew, Richmond and
Hampton Court
Where the kestrel soars
Near a plane that roars
To a swarm over
Heathrow Airport

And the hawk squawks in a squall
Of rain
And dives to the river,
Over Kew Bridge

Over the Richmond train
Gliding into Central London
Over neighbourhoods watching
While their hands, they are washing
After hanging
The dirty linen out to dry
In the window-mirrored heat
Of microchip city
Where big and little fish fry
And without any pity
A new brutality breachloads fears
Lays plans and hatches smears
Media-sedated, computer-dated
Trapped, wrapped and sealed
Caught in electronic nets
Branded, cracked
All privacy unpeeled

And high in the dusty sky
An artificial comet glimmers
Snooping like a spy
Through an infrared telescope eye
As the kestrel, poised on high
Flaps its wings
Ignoring commotion below
That car light and street light
Illuminates brashly bright
As the sky light
Gradually dissipates
Turning wings are
Whirling in the winds
Returning to a feathered dream
Of darting over a mountain stream

In the hovering stillness of sleep
Across the bleary twilight sky
Of a twilight nation
To the IBM tower
At Gunnersbury station.

Steve Tasane has been dealing in class A literature for the last decade with a series of one-man shows, as promoter with the groundbreaking Apples & Snakes (1993–97) and as co-founder of poetry's first pop group, Atomic Lip. The Lip kick-started the populist Litpop movement, putting together the seminal three-day LITPOP98 festival at the 100 Club. He explodes the myth of poetry's elitism by performing at venues such as Dingwalls, Ronnie Scott's and the Glastonbury Jazz Stage. His first collection, *Bleeding Heart*, was published by Gecko Press in 1996. '[*Sic*]', his post-modern montage of sampled literature, was the first example of the 'performance novel'.

Bleeding Heart

Love is
anathema to logic
Love is aimless revolution
Love will cure the phobia
& though instils an inner peace
form a laughter line from every troubled frown
without the coming down Love is an umbrella when there isn't any rain
a aromatic massage when there isn't any pain   Love is weeping eye
eye Love is double glazing Love is a vicious hellcat fight & sycophantic
ising Love is as stubborn as the stain that even Persil can't remove
ve is a scratchy Motown track the dirty needle in the groove
ve makes a mug of tea in bed the morning after
oozing Love is setting lovers free while
ubliminally accusing Love is late for work again
Love is looking glam the best thing in the universe
& a good-for-nothing sham Love is kissing under moonlight
Love is sex on a train Love connects the bleeding heart to the
throbbing vein Love is life's lubricant Love is 4 legs in a
bath Love makes 2 individuals a single psychopath Love
is a triple figure phone bill Love will strike us dumb it
leads to lavish poetry to which we all succumb Love is very
complicated Love is black & white it might be
paradoxical but always love is right Love is
bloodyminded Love is strong
& true Love is unafraid of
cliche & Love is
me & you

Love is
lateral & wild
Love is 9 to 5 reviled
but give us sweaty palms
is yet a call to arms Love will
Love is nature's Prozac

Tim Turnbull was born in Scarborough, North Yorkshire in 1960. He has been a forestry labourer for nearly twenty years, and self-employed for most of these. He started writing poetry in the late seventies, and gave it up to play in a load of punk, ska and industrial bands and then started writing again in the early '90s. Since then he has toured the US twice with slam teams, in '96 and '98, performed at festivals and clubs all over Britain and Ireland and contributed regularly to magazines (most frequently to the *Rising* series). In 1998 he was a prize-winner of the National Poetry Competition and graduated from Middlesex University in 1999.

Raw Horse

I step into the restaurant

> And bellow my order
> Bellow my order

Bring me a raw horse
Bring me a horse I roar!

> Waiter!

Bring me a whole horse
Bring me a whole live horse!

> Waiter!

The other customers quail
Bewildered children clutch their mothers' skirts
And wail

The maitre d'
Whimpers, smiles a nervous smile
And sidles up to me

'P'haps M'sieur would laak to traa
Som escalope of veal
Smothered in a rich waan sauce
With 'aricots vert
Et pommes Dauphinoise . . .'

NO! BRING ME A HORSE

An uneasy murmur ripples
                              Round the room
As diners shuffle knives and forks
                                      And spoons
The air is dense with desperation
                                    And gloom
They're hoping it'll all be over
                              Soon
They glance
              About
   For a way
                 To escape
              Then

One man panics and makes a break
I intercept him with a body check
That drives him through the plate glass shopfront
He dies impaled in a pool on the pavement

NOW NOBODY MOVE
TILL I FINISH MY FOOD

And bring me a raw horse
Bring me a horse I roar
                    Waiter!

The horse is brought
It shies and struggles and stamps and snorts
I strip to the waist
The waiter trips and stumbles
In his haste to get away

He crashes through the kitchen doors
Which clatter on their springs revealing
The sous-chef swinging by his apron strings
From a hook in the kitchen ceiling

My sinews strain and muscles flex
Flecks of foam from the horse's nostrils
Spatter my chest

A couple of pensioners piss their pants
And with a screech beseech me
'Oh spare the noble beast
Eat us instead
We're old and bony
But our blood is red.
Oh spare the horse'
The pair implore.

Two well aimed fish forks
Nail them to the wall

The air is thick with sweat
And fear
The horse's eyes roll white
It screams and rears.

I grasp its head
And taking care to bite an ear off
While it's still alive,
I wrestle it to the floor

Tables, chairs are splintered
Crockery breaks
I snap its neck
Its legs keep flailing
As I tear into its flesh

Eating, eating, eating, eating,
Eating, eating, eating,
Eating, eating,
Eating

Till I'm sated.

Then when gorged
I torch the place
And walk away
Covered head to toe
In guts and gore.

Because I eat horses

I eat horses

I eat horses

RAW ....

'With the Breakdown of Faith in the Established Churches and
the Collapse of Confidence in the Certainties of the Enlight-
enment, We in the Western World, at the End of the Twentieth
Century, have Witnessed a Curious Blurring of the Boundaries
between Art, Science and Religion.' Discuss.

That's as maybe.
I've been thinking about something similar
lately, at least where writers are concerned,
and I've concluded that the novelists' craft
is not unlike that branch of behavioural
science –

     the one where scientists persuade
day-old fluffy ducklings that their mothers
are battery-operated robots, or beach balls,
or some such, then film the tweeting creatures
tumbling over one another, trying to find
a wing to shelter under, in acute and evident
distress.

     Or the one where they build plastic
rat-cities, populate them with lab-rats,
then introduce viruses or engender
tumours on the beasts' backs. And observe.
And fill clipboards with notes on mortality
rates, population dynamics, aggression
or group relationships and then extrapolate
dubious conclusions about the human
condition.

     Our own art, which some still call
Poesy, is more analogous with, I think,
the vivisectionist's trade. Turning something
furry and familiar inside out;

exposing guts, gills, livers, lungs and a clutch
of unborn young, all infused with the stink
of alcohol and death. God have mercy on us.
                    Somebody get me a drink.

'To be sure, in **Christopher Twigg**'s poems, you can catch a semblance of perfectly normal first-person poetry: small happenings tweaked into significance, the world's impact attentively felt, efficient similes, word-play and sound-effects, down-beat ends. But the tight lip, the face-saving face that this poetry often presents, is absent.

He's something of a New Age seeker, a self-help salvationist. He bonds with nature, and extends his sympathy to all things living and non-living. He visits his mother in the country. He makes journeys in a spirit of pilgrimage. He marks festivals. He gets miserable. He lives in London. He is a single man. And he sings of himself because he finds in his experience many occasions for growth, connection, blessing, revelation, which he would have us share.' Tom Lubbock, from the introduction to *In the Chair*, by Christopher Twigg (Alces Press, 1997).

Brittany Ferries

Spring finds me on the car deck
where I lie like a cigarette end
relishing my freedom.
Behind me a Spanish school party
study the constellations.

My bunk has pink sheets
and a ladder to reach it.
A corduroy crimson sofa,
a shower and a basin
with threads of vomit that the cleaners missed.

I visit *Captain Colin's Magic Show*
for boys and girls under seven
full of innuendo
he has wands that droop and mysteriously erect themselves,
balloons with teats,
a handkerchief that gathers like a tentpole.

I stand among the grown ups beyond glass
in the *Yacht Club* bar. The setting sun
is an egg yolk
softly added to the sea's cocktail.
A boy they've dressed as Tarzan flexes his muscles.
The rising moon has water on the brain,
hydrocephalic —
It staggers naked like a zombie
through the streets of Milwaukee.

Here in this floating hospital
with *Chanel* and *Fabergé* counters,
I request songs from the pianist, wintering.
I can't remember anything.
My name is Christopher. My toothmug came
wrapped in plastic. The bedpan is stained
as if it had been fried
too long by accident.
The Captain has asked me
to turn my lights out at night
so he can navigate.
Spray and woodland then ice
and bare rock.
On the third morning I wake
to snow on the roofs of the lorries.

To The Round Moon

Round moon you come to my window
like a pregnant belly or a searchlight
to verify my activities
to check all's well
with my television licence and my neighbours.
You are as detached and efficient as a therapist
or McDonalds employee.
You wear a white coat like a surgeon
and clear the dead wasps from my drawers.

Welcome moon to shine in on my house and life.
All's pure in here you'll find.
No filthy poppies do enseam
my moon bed, my moon armchair,
my moon boots with the compass hidden in the heel.
All's *lunar* here you'll find.

Oh moon, dogfish cold and unshaven,
I saw you loaded into vans at Finisterre.
By your light the French camera crew video the Kaffir dancers,
the heroin is smuggled successfully into Dover,
the seaweed reaches the surface at double its usual rate.
I call upon you now
to bless my friend Adam
and guide him safe to Compostela.

Note on *Compostela:* My 'friend' Adam was walking the long-distance path
to Santiago de Compostela in Galicia at the time I wrote this poem
(November 1992). *Compostela* comes from *Campo de la Estrella* which means
'field of the star'.

To My Feet

My dear and holy feet five feet away
with shadowed valleys dark between the toes;
you love to walk over the rich spring grass,
or wet sea sand . . .
I call you 'the warm outposts
of my loving Self at rest'.

When I was in hospital
a lady photographer came
and photographed my feet.
Maybe they've saved lives!
by helping doctors
identify the rash
of meningitis.

Big toes move in shoes
like molluscs.
Nails tender as moons
arch under leather.

When I lost my faith
my feet never doubted;
they kept up a groundswell
of firm belief.
When I cursed God and Nature
and wanted to die
my feet were sorry as tree trunks
when the birds go hungry.

Compassionate extremities!
Lovers of carpet and meadow!
Breaking the crust of snow and sinking in!
Delighting in the sand's resilience!
Heels scuffing circles; toes
stubbed painfully on driftwood.

(You, concrete pavements, when will you respond,
draw back, or even recognize my feet?)
Oh let me not ignore their happiness,
their life of present moments, felt and lived!
How can I but repay their teaching than
with walks through sea, with walks on sand or grass?

Tim Wells lives in N16 where he edits the *Rising* series. He likes Chinese food, bluegrass music and fondly remembers the water margins of Liang Shan Po.

And Too Many Byrds' Records

Love seeps from me
it steams in my piss
it flakes in my snot
it stinks in my sweat
Love is so much a part of me
that I could no more shit it out
than I could stop my heart from beating
Love is my sustenance
my breakfast
lunch
and dinner
it is my water
beer
and spirit
I breathe its breath
wear its apparel
walk within its furrow
and live in its abundance
I feel love's colour on my face
This is no drug talking
This is me
who put his shoulder to the world
This is me
trying hard to be better

Andy White, was born and grew up in Belfast, Northern Ireland. He wrote his first poem entitled 'Riots' when he was nine and picked up a guitar aged thirteen after hearing John Lennon singing 'Give Peace A Chance'. After leaving school, Andy read English at Cambridge and travelled down to London with his acoustic guitar and a suitcase full of poetry. 'Religious Persuasion', his first single, came out on Stiff Records in 1985 and started his musical career. His first solo album, *Rave on Andy White*, was released worldwide in 1986. Since then Andy has returned to Ireland, recorded five more solo albums, toured the world and won Ireland's top songwriting award. His latest release is a 'Best of' collection entitled *andywhite compilation*. A companion volume to this is *The Music of What Happens*, Andy's book of collected song lyrics, poems and drawings, which is published in Ireland by Lagan Press. Andy currently resides in Switzerland with his wife Christine and their son Sebastian.

Beautiful Girl Walks Out of the Bar

1.
When a beautiful girl
walks out of the bar
it's always a shame
especially
if you were with
the beautiful girl
walking out of the bar

2.
When a beautiful girl
walks out of the bar
morale drops generally

3.
Wonder what it's like
waking up
a beautiful girl
looking in the mirror
and it looks back beautiful

4.
When a beautiful girl
walks out of the bar
bad news for fans
of the beautiful girl
good news for
the street outside

5.
When a beautiful girl
walks out of the bar
her boyfriend looks at the bill
give it to me
I'll pay it

6.
Some people think poems
are about eagles
trumpets
subtle shades of diction
yeah
that's all good stuff
but they're also about
a beautiful girl
walking out of a bar

7.
That's it
she's history
the beautiful girl
just walked out of the bar
strange
how they don't just
shut up shop
when that happens

Up Down

When we were young
I remember coming down from Belfast to Dublin
on the train and later in a battered red Renault 4
for a treat

we went to the Dandelion Market
where you could buy beads and
there were strange smells and kaftans
and once we saw a group with a
singer standing on the PA speakers
I wonder who that was

there was me and my girlfriend from school
she was really called Roxy
because at that time
there were a lot of people
suddenly being called Roxy

we went to No Romance and bought
red and black striped trousers
you never saw in Belfast
and we were shy going in the shop
and into Peter's Pub for underage Guinness
and ham sandwiches

when we were young
I remember coming down from Belfast to Dublin
on the train and later in a battered red Renault 4
for a treat
and the sun shone down on Grafton Street
because it was always in the summer

coffee at Bewley's
buying jeans with lots of pockets
we did all the tourist things
because when we were young
I remember coming down from Belfast to Dublin
on the train and later in a battered red Renault 4
for a treat

and in Dublin there were no troubles because
just as on the way down they were stripped away
on the long road home
Drogheda was the Battle of the Boyne
there was a Sinn Fein office on Dundalk main street
no man's land is dark at night
a checkpoint and a car showroom of grey jeeps
at Newry police station
and written on a Belfast wall was
'We shall never forsake the blue skies of Ulster
for the grey mists of an Irish republic'

and we never believed it
because the sun shone down on Grafton Street
because it was always in the summer

when we were young
I remember coming down from Belfast to Dublin
on the train and later in a battered red Renault 4
for a treat

Hugo Williams was born in Windsor in 1942 and grew up in Sussex. He worked on the *London Magazine* from 1961 to 1970, since when he has earned his living as a journalist and travel writer (*No Particular Place To Go*, Jonathan Cape, 1980). He was TV critic on the *New Statesman* and theatre critic on the *Sunday Correspondent*. He currently writes the 'Freelance' column in the *TLS*.

His first book of poetry was *Writing Home* (OUP, 1985), followed by *Selected Poems* (OUP, 1989), *Dock Leaves* (Faber & Faber, 1994) and *Billy's Rain* (Faber & Faber, 1999). He lives in London.

Her News

You paused for a moment and I heard you smoking
on the other end of the line.
I pictured your expression,
one eye screwed shut against the smoke
as you waited for my reaction.
I was waiting for it myself, a list of my own news
gone suddenly cold in my hand.
Supposing my wife found out, what would happen then?
Would I have to leave her and marry you now?

Perhaps it wouldn't be so bad,
starting again with someone new, finding a new place,
pretending the best was yet to come.
It might even be fun,
playing the family man, walking around in the park
full of righteous indignation.
But no, I couldn't go through all that again,
not without my own wife being there,
not without her getting cross about everything.

Perhaps she wouldn't mind about the baby,
then we could buy a house in the country
and all move in together.
That sounded like a better idea.
Now that I'd been caught at last, a wave of relief
swept over me. I was just considering
a shed in the garden with a radio and a day bed,
when I remembered I hadn't seen you for over a year.
'Congratulations,' I said. 'When's it due?'

Robbie Williams was born in 1974 in Newcastle-under-Lyme. He joined Take That at sixteen and was with the band during eight of their No. 1 hits. After leaving the band in 1995 he pursued a solo career and was signed to Chrysalis Records in '96.

His debut album, *Life Thru a Lens*, first entered the album charts at No. 11 and became a No. 1 hit on its 26th week of release. On entering the Top 10 the LP remained there for forty weeks. The album is now certified at 6 × platinum in the UK and re-entered the top ten in the first chart of 1999. His second album, *I've Been Expecting You*, was released in October 1998 and is also certified at 7 × platinum and returned to No. 1 in the first chart of 1999.

He recently won Brit awards for best single with 'Angels', for best video with 'Millennium' and for 'Best Male Artist'. This poem was written by Robbie when he was sixteen years old.

Hello Sir

Hello Sir, remember me?
I'm the man you thought I'd never be
The boy who you reduced to tears
Lad called 'thingy' for six whole years.

Yes that's right, my name's Bob
The one who landed the pop star's job
The one who you told, look don't touch
The kid who doesn't amount to much

Well, I'm here and you're still there
With a fake sports car and receding hair.
Dodgy Farah trousers that think you are smart
Married to the woman that teaches art.

Married to the life, married to the school
I wanna sing and dance sir, now who's the fool?
Sing and dance, you thought I was barmy,
Settle down 'thingy', join the army.

And who are you to tell me this?
The dream I want I'll have to miss
Sir is God, he's been given the right
To structure lives overnight.

Now I know life's true path,
Tanks and guns that'll be a laugh.
No, not me I'm a mega civilian
I won't lead my life riding pillion.

But thanks for the advice and I'm sure it'll do
For negative dick heads just like you.
As for now I've a different weapon
Stage and screen is about to beckon.

And here I sit in first class, bollocks sir, kiss my arse . . .

Kevin Williamson was born in the sixties and lives and works in Edinburgh. His occupations have included: trainee nuclear scientist, cocktail barman, door-to-door salesman, journalist, library gopher, pool shark, adult education tutor, and now editor of the Rebel Inc. imprint of Canongate Books. He founded, edited and published *Rebel Inc* magazine from 1992–96 and co-wrote *A Visitor's Guide To Edinburgh* with Irvine Welsh in 1993. He launched the Scotland Against Drugs Hypocrisy campaign in 1996. His first book, *Drugs And The Party Line*, was published in October 1996, and his short story 'Heart of the Bass' appeared in *Disco Biscuits* (Sceptre) the following year.

Advising A Philistine

The venereal scribe,
barrel spent and satisfied,
lays down his gun
and yawns of owls and cats
and romantic comedies.

The fans rise to their feet,
shaking the stadium, singing:
'There's only one washed-up poet . . .
one washed up po-yet . . .'

I add my own tuppence worth:
Ahem . . .
easy rhymes are no highway
to the complexities of the human soul.
There is a yearn beyond
metrics, comparison and wit.
And fuck the rich.

Is that so, he sneers.

Aye.

Anything else?

Aye . . .
if in doubt, leave it out.

Pottering around his house
he tends to his metaphors
but says nothing.

You know, it would be churlish
to hand him a cheese-grater
to scrape away
at the thin veneer of meaning.

One Down

Your voice was soft and hesitant,
the door a perfect frame for
the lemon twist of your words:

'Could you at least put down the
paper and listen to what I'm saying.
The crossword can wait.'

Conjugal Join? Mental cogs whirred
as I sifted through the swamp of
consonants and vowels. *Conjugal Join?*

'I've had enough. I'm leaving. If space is
what you want, then space is what you've
got. But you'll have to fill it without me.'

The words echoed empty in the hall. I heard
a taxi door slam in the distance. Of course!
Colloquial slang. Four letters. As in off.

Andy Willoughby was born in 1965 in Scarborough and grew up on a council estate near the docks and the steelworks in Middlesbrough. After taking a degree in English at the University of Kent, where he was awarded the TS Eliot prize for poetry in 1986, and a Masters in Theatre at Sheffield, he now works as an occasional teacher and most frequently as a struggling poet and playwright.

Word Experience

Stages of progression – kitted out in quick succession
With steel cap boots safety hats and a copy of the rules
Then it was work from eight till four fetching and carrying tools
Shovelling shit for the men on the factory floor

During tea-break we gained access to the macho ranks
Laughing at crude jokes about women
When the most we'd had was a clumsy grope or quick wank
Behind the school canteen at the Christmas dance

What chance did we have to realise the world
We thought was ours was built for someone else's joy
When our only words were not our choice
All that 'Tits' and 'Fuck that' amidst deafening noise

From the great machine which we served as parts
'Ah've got me spanner and me nuts to break some hearts'
I tried to piece the words together find a different sense
No 'dirty cunts' no 'slaggy tarts' that false defence

After work running home to wash off stains of sweat and oil
Sitting alone sipping beer hands lusting after fresh pages
In new books for words that would not oppress or soil or twist
Only when we make words ours can we speak of love and
    sexual bliss.

Volleying The Invisible

We played football in the gloaming
Enacting home international glories
Not even stopping with the sunset
When the ball disappeared into deadlight

I still hear the backbeat of your kick
and the echo of my swung anticipation
You're England and I'm Northern Ireland
Being the better fighter you take the lion's choice

But I improved there in the darkness
Listening intensely for the unseen
Today I haven't lost that precious habit
Though if I were to strike the ball now

It would end up in older hands
Work worn red and laced with scars
While mine are pale pen-pushers
Still striving for that sweet connection

Our feet made from beat to striking beat
Although we never meet these days
John, I still strive to impress you
Volleying the invisible into imagination's net.

Nicky Wire was born in 1969 in Tredegar, South Wales and was educated at Oakdale Comprehensive, Cross Keys College and Swansea University. After a two-week stint as a postman he got together with some old childhood friends and formed The Manic Street Preachers.
Nicky loves painting, walking and sport and lives with his wife Rachel and their dog in South Wales.

A Prologue To History

WERE WE THE KINNOCK FACTOR
AM I TALKING PRIVATE SECTOR
DO I THINK I'M SHAUN WILLIAM RYDER
OR MY FORMER FRIEND WHO'S NOW UNDERCOVER
HE'S GONE AND I'M NO DESERTER
PERHAPS I'M HARD ALL THE SAME

TODAY A POET WHO CAN'T PLAY GUITAR
TOMORROW STEVE OVETT HAS INJURED HIS CALF
NEXT YEAR THE WORLD'S GREATEST POLITICIAN
YESTERDAY THE BOY WHO ONCE HAD A MISSION
I DON'T WANT TO BE
A PROLOGUE TO HISTORY

SO I WATER MY PLANTS WITH EVIAN
A BRAND NEW DYSON THAT IS DECADENT
READ MY PAPERS AND THE BUSINESS SECTION
CHECKOUT THE TESSAS AND THE PENSIONS
PHONE MY FRIENDS AND THEY'RE ALRIGHT
SO I PRAY FOR THE SAFETY OF THE NIGHT

REMEMBER ETHNIC CLEANSING IN THE HIGHLANDS
NO ONE SAYS A THING IN THE MIDDLE OF
   EN-GER-LAND
I'M BRUISED FRUIT BUT STILL TASTE SO NICE
BUT IF YOU LOOK AT ME YOU BETTER LOOK TWICE
I'M TALKING RUBBISH TO COVER UP THE CRACKS
AN EMPTY VESSEL WHO CAN'T MAKE CONTACT

TODAY A POET WHO CAN'T PLAY GUITAR
TOMORROW PHIL BENNET'S PLAYING OUTSIDE HALF
NEXT YEAR THE WORLD'S GREATEST POLITICIAN
YESTERDAY THE BOY WHO ONCE HAD A MISSION

I DON'T WANT TO BE
A PROLOGUE TO HISTORY, A PROLOGUE
TO HISTORY

My Little Empire

MY LITTLE EMPIRE
HAS RISEN AND IT'S SET
MY LITTLE EMPIRE
IS AS GOOD AS IT CAN GET
MY LITTLE EMPIRE
IS COMING AROUND
MY LITTLE EMPIRE
IT DON'T MAKE A SOUND

MY ROYALTY
IT DOES NOT EXIST
IT IS EXTINCT

FOR THE EYE TO SEE
MY IDEOLOGY
IT IS DEAD AND GONE
ALMOST FORGOTTEN
FOR THE EYE TO SEE

MY LITTLE EMPIRE
I'M SICK OF BEING SICK
MY LITTLE EMPIRE
I'M TIRED OF BEING TIRED
MY LITTLE EMPIRE
I'M BORED OF BEING BORED
MY LITTLE EMPIRE
I'M HAPPY BEING SAD

ALL OF MY SINS ARE ATTEMPTS TO FILL VOIDS
ALL OF MY VOIDS THEY ARE FILLED WITH SIN
ALL OF MY DEMONS THEY ARE KEPT WITHIN
AND ALL MY VIOLENCE IT DOES NOT EXIST

MY LITTLE EMPIRE
I'M HAPPY BEING SAD
MY LITTLE EMPIRE
I'M FUCKED WITH BEING FUCKED
MY LITTLE EMPIRE
I'M DONE WITH BEING DUMB
MY LITTLE EMPIRE
I'M HAPPY BEING SAD
HAPPY BEING SAD
HAPPY BEING SAD
HAPPY BEING SAD

Murray Lachlan Young's verse is concerned with the foibles of our modern age, a world of debauchery, excess and fading morality. His cautionary tales articulate action and consequence, influenced by the children's verses of Hilaire Belloc and Heinrich Hoffman. Where Belloc talked of gluttony and dangerous toys, Young writes about cocaine and even more dangerous toys. He is also very funny.

Live, Young breaks the conventions of poetry readings, both in style and his choice of venue; experimenting with musical accompaniment (from Brix Smith to classical cello) and is equally at home in Madame Jo Jo's or the Purcell Rooms.

Following the success of his album *Vice and Verse* (EMI), his first book of poetry entitled *Casual Sex and Other Verse* was published in October 1997 by Bantam Books.

The Life & Death of Art

Half man half prawn reclining on a corned-beef chaise longue
Yes, contemporary art is what I speak of
And half man half prawn was its searing blade
Until one balmy night near the end of high summer
A new ace was pulled from the tumbling deck
A trump card produced and then cunningly played.

The gallery was rammed and buzzing
In high expectation of what was to come
Some said an act of pure existentialism
Others a mixture of Dada and Jung
There had been some confusion just by the main door
For a Shih Tzu had laid a small turd on the floor
Hence a group from the art school
Had left their depression

Declaring a spontaneous act of expression
In short it was just too avant-garde
The rumours were running like molten lard.

Did the sperm come from Dali
The egg from Fonteyn
The artist-cum-surgeon
A fast-breaking name
The surrogate mother knew what was expected
For her broken waters had been shaken and stirred
By the funky bartender so cool and connected
Frankincense burned as the dour dilettante
Sipped on his cool embryonic frappe
The heavily pregnant birth mother entered
And a bearded philanthropist shouted 'Ole!'
Murmurs rose as she stepped on the canvas
Clad in polyandrous birthing smock
A guru's low mantra rang out from the Tannoy
(Nam myoho renge kyo)
The lights were dimmed low until but one single spot
Illuminated the birth of the innocent child.

Tiny silent bright on bare white canvas
An act of creation quite second to none
Tiny silent bright on bare white canvas
Unaware of its role in a cruel world to come.

Tarquin Mule the artist-cum-surgeon
Stepped forward and snipped the umbilical cord
Then adjusting his black raw-silk surgeon's gown
Held the child aloft as though addressing the Lord

'I proclaim this child to be all that is art
And all that is art to be this child
Its name will be Art
And so will its nature
So let's kick off the bidding
In the honour of Nietzsche.'

Pepe Le Blanc the celebrity chef
Bore the afterbirth off on a cold silver tray
The birth mother sedated was put in a car
As he feverishly started to flip and flambe
And by the time he had served up his radically chic canape
The bloodstained canvas and baby boy
Had been snapped up and wrapped up and driven away.

Art's life was brief and uninspiring
Because everything Art touched turned to art
Fifty soiled nappies behind tinted Perspex
His first work sold for the price of a theme park
Schooled in a gallery cut from glass
A contemporary mariner tied to the mast
Of his life on a windless sea
Poor Art became lonely as lonely can be.

By the age of twenty he'd grossed twelve billion
But at last found love with a girl named Vermilion
Who ran her own public relations firm
The promotion of art was its sole concern.

She told him he was a living god
And fed him with pink analgesic pills
She told him whatever he wanted to hear

(She was in PR for Christ's sake, it was her job)
And Art paid the bills.

But oh what a day
What a catastrophic shock
When Art returned home from his self-help group
To find his bedroom door firmly locked
The Bentley estate parked behind the wall
The half-empty bottle of vintage Krug
The surgeon's gown on the floor in the hall
He peeked through the keyhole
His heart in his throat
To see Vermilion in flagrante delicto
Tied hand and foot
With a raw-silk rope.

The co-respondent it was plain to see
Was Tarquin Mule, his mentor, creator
Yes, Tarquin Mule, that villainous fiend.

On a dark and dusty old factory floor
Art first shed his clothes before bolting the door
He mounted the gibbet of improvised crates
Contemplating his life in its tragic fate
He tied up the noose, said a short prayer
Broken-hearted, spent and ruined
He closed his dull eyes
Then kicked the cold air.

But the instant he did
Twenty floodlights flashed on
And surrounded he was by a chattering throng

Of champagne-sipping bourgeoisie
Art critics, socialites, national TV and radio crews
All there to peruse
But most disgustingly
Most disgracefully
Most outrageously
Tarquin Mule
Powdered and Cruel
Hemp-clad and nimble
Jumped up on a stool.

'Witness my friends, the death of Art'
(Tarquin spoke working the room like a tart)
With a snap of his fingers
A black canvas was laid
Beneath poor twitching Art
For his swansong to play.

It is said the last motion of a hanging man
Is ejaculation
And there according to Tarquin's heinous plan
The last drops of life
Spilt forth from Art's trembling form
Hit the canvas stark and bare
There in death
His last work was born.

The exhibition lasted ninety days
Whilst Art turned green and rotted away
Tarquin and Vermilion moved to LA
And still live there now I've heard people say.

So the moral is clear and the moral is plain
In this case I'm afraid only art is to blame
So believe what you wish
Or believe who you are
But please make sure above all else
That you never ever ever believe in your own PR.

The Cyber Tragedy

(To be spoken in a German accent)

I don't go out I just stay in and I go to the cyber café.
I meet all my friends and have such a good time
when I go to the cyber café.
Last year I went to a cyber disco
it was really a lot of fun.
I danced the whole night with a wonderful girl
who looked just like Pamela Anderson. Well, virtually.

Yeah we fell for each other and got virtually drunk,
then had virtual sex in the back of her car.
She e-mailed and said she was virtually pregnant
and never intended to go quite so far.
What could I do? I virtually loved her
I did the virtually decent thing.
We were wed in a cyber chapel of love
I gave her my virtual diamond ring.

I felt so happy I virtually cried
I told all my friends at the cyber café

I wed the most wonderful virtual girl on this virtually
wonderful day.

But news came back and I was virtually sick
for my bride I was told by my virtual best friend
was known as a virtual serial bigamist
married to three thousand other men.

I nearly virtually killed myself.
I nearly virtually strung myself up.
I came close to joining a cyber monastery
becoming a virtual monk.

But then it got worse.
It got much, much worse.
For a terrible thing had gone undetected
we'd taken no proper precautions
I'd left my modem unprotected!
I was struck down by a virtual virus.
It scrambled my data and wiped my disk.
I felt such a virtual idiot,
but I'd no real excuse for I'd known all the risks.

Now I just weep by my keyboard
surrounded in despondency shrouded in gloom.
But, as Mother says: 'Things can't be . . . really . . . so bad.'
Because if I don't want to
I never really need come out of my bedroom.

Benjamin Zephaniah was born in Birmingham, and grew up in Jamaica and in Handsworth, where he was sent to an approved school for being rebellious and 'a born failure', ending up in jail for burglary. After prison he turned from crime to music and poetry. In 1989 he was nominated to be Oxford Professor of Poetry.

Cybersex

I heard dat out in cyberspace
There is a very special place
Where you can go and have a taste
Of three-dimensional love.

When I heard dis I said all right
I have to taste this new delight
I had to find that love web site
For three-dimensional love.

I found a hacker jacking-in
With a friendly server serving him
I surf because I cannot swim
For three-dimensional love.

My modem waz performing fine
The clock said it was cybertime
All my emotions went on line
For three-dimensional love.

In virtual reality
The database waz dating me
I still kept my virginity
For three-dimensional love.

High without any narcotics
In search of some cyberotics
I search through all related topics
On three-dimensional love.

I found it, it was so attractive
Its interface was just perfective
And we got very interactive
On three-dimensional love.

I felt my mouse go wild and spasm
This is not no pleonasm
We blew a great big cyborgasm
Sweet three-dimensional love.

Acknowledgements

'E (Manic Dance Mix A)' and 'It's Better Post- Than Pre-' first
appeared in *R.A.W.* (Gecko Press, 1995). © Patience
Agbabi 1995

'John XXVII' and 'Blind Worms' © Rich Beale 1999

'All Of The Goodness, None Of The Mess' and 'The Poem That
Was Really A List' were both first published in *Rising*
magazine. 'The Poem That Was Really A List' was also
published in *Gargoyle* issue No. 41. © Francesca Beard
1999

'79 Kingfield', 'Waiting For My Mother' and 'Dating' first
appeared in *Terrifying Ordeal* (Hearing Eye, 1998). © Paul
Birtill 1999

'My Sister': words by David Boulter © Rough Trade Publishing
Ltd 1996

'Sonnet IX' first appeared in *Maiden Speech* (Bloodaxe Books,
1996). © Eleanor Brown 1996

'Drums and Flags', 'Chelsea vs Pablo Picasso' and 'The Ugly'
© Joe Cairo 1999

'Time Jesum Transeuntum Et Non Revertentum' and 'Nobody's
Baby Now' first appeared in *King Ink II* (Black Spring Press,
1997) Nick Cave and The Bad Seeds, available on Mute
Records. © Mute Song Ltd 1997

'Family Way' first appeared in *No Other Blue* (Penguin Books Ltd,
1998). © Craig Charles 1998

'The Bitter Cup' first appeared on the LP *At The Bridge* performed by Billy Childish with The Singing Loins and released in 1993 through Damaged Goods. © Billy Childish 1993

'You Make Me Die' first appeared on the album *Acropolis Now* performed by Thee Mighty Caesars and released in 1986 on Milkshake Records. © Billy Childish 1986

'The Library of Love' © John Citizen 1999

'Helen's Boyfriend', 'Last Orders' and 'Art' first appeared in *Sacrilege* (Bloodaxe Books, 1998). © Brendan Cleary 1998

'Deep Fried in Kelvin' is taken from the B-side to the twelve inch vinyl *Lipgloss*: Cocker, Senior, Banks, Mackey and Doyle with lyrics by Jarvis Cocker. Published by Island Music Ltd. © Island Records 1994

'Have You Met Clive D'Arcy(?)' and 'I Wouldn't Shoot You' © Andrew Copeman 1999

'Piano, Window, Piano' © Stuart David 1999

'Giro Day' © Jegsy Dodd 1999

'The Blackest Man In The Universe' © David Duff 1999

'Ae Want Ti Be', 'Politiks Ae Kissin' and 'Enterprise' © Sandie Craigie 1999

'Cuttin' Legs', 'Burial' and 'Handgun' © Raoul Kawalsky 1999

'I Wiz Nearly A Daddy Once' © Ray Myles 1999

'Safer Steps' © Anrew Edwards 1999

'Let Me Be', 'Liar' and 'Make Me A Modern Christian Song' © Lucy English 1999

'Hey! Hey! – Pinochet!', 'Advice To Mothers' and 'Poem About A Man Whose Wife Leaves Him For Good' © Lloyd Evans 1999

'The Pet' first appeared in *All Alcoholics Are Charmers* (Anvil Press Poetry Ltd, 1998). © Martina Evans 1998

'Jack The Biscuit' © Andy Fairley 1999

'To The Man With The Hair' and 'TV Ladies' © Salena Saliva Godden 1999

'Lunchtime Sandwich Secretaries' and 'Nero' first appeared on the album *Poems, Speeches, Thoughts and Doodles* released by Science Friction 1997. © Roy Harper 1999

'My Great Life', 'Riot Girl' and 'Better Drinker' © Fay Hart 1999

'Stoned': words and Music by Polly Jean Harvey © 1999, Hot Head Music Ltd. Reproduced by permission of EMI Music Publishing Ltd, London WC2H 0EA.

'One Line': words and music by Polly Jean Harvey © 1999, Hot Head Music Ltd. Reproduced by permission of EMI Music Publishing Ltd, London WC2H 0EA.

'Tape Y/r Head On' © Control 1999

'Jimmy Clitheroe's Penis' © Damien Hirst and Joe Strummer 1999

'Burials' and 'At This Time' © Adam Horovitz 1999

'Dust' © Scott Martingell 1999

'Rio Song' and 'The Road Less Travelled' © Alan Jenkins 1999

'manscape' and 'Anima Mundi – World Soul' © Patrick Jones 1999

'Why' © Vic Lambrusco 1999

'An Educated Guess' first appeared in the collection *Scars and Stripes* (Golden Handshake, 1997). © Fran Landesman 1997

'The Usual Suspects' and 'If We're So Hip' © Fran Landesman 1998

'Post Human' and 'Goodbye' © Anna Landucci 1999

'Round The Bridging Table' © Betsy de Lotbinière 1999

'Trophy Bimbo', 'Lovey' and 'Summer Girl' © Sarah-Jane Lovett 1999

'Acid' and 'My Pain' © Roddy Lumsden 1999

'It's Cool In Goole' first appeared in *Evolver* (Do Me A Favour and Favour, 1997). © Paul Lyalls 1997

'Hands Of The Barmaid', 'Pinned Down' *and* 'The Dunes' © Shane MacGowan/Perfect Songs Ltd 1999

'Tell Me' and 'Mummy' © Amber Marks 1999

'I'm Not Bitter' and 'Cunts' by Arab Strap with lyrics by Aidan
    Moffat © Arab Strap 1999

'Time passed unnoticed until she took the clock' first appeared in
    Nude Modelling for the Afterlife (Bloodaxe Books, 1993).
    © Henry Normal 1993

'Ex-Hippies' first appeared in *Unlike The Buddha* (Jackson's Arm,
    1997). © Nigel Planer 1997

'A Friday Night At The End Of A Millennium' first appeared in
    The Heavy-Petting Zoo (Bloodaxe Books, 1998). © Clare
    Pollard 1998

'Shedding Skin' © Martin Preston 1999

'I Am Not An Alcoholic' © James Raiher 1999

'Irish Lassies Shag Like Fuck' and 'Victim Of A Miracle' © Paul
    Reekie 1999

'Lamentation For Stephen' and 'Memoir' © Roger Robinson
    1999

'I'd Rather Be Dead' © Jem Rolls 1999

'Burton's First XV' and 'My Stags and Hens Mobile Disco'
    © Gareth Sager 1999

'Boy' and 'Red Hot Lust' © Chris Savage King 1999

'Thunder Over Kilburn', 'R.N.L.I.' and 'Nectarine No. 9'
    © Jock Scot 1999

'BMW' © Brinsley Sheridan 1999

'I Love London' and 'How High Can A Kestral Fly?' © Paul
    Stewart 1999

'Bed Island' © Hank Starrs 1999

'Bleeding Heart' © Steve Tasane 1999

'Raw Horse' and 'That's As Maybe' © Tim Turnbull 1999

'Brittany Ferries' first appeared in *In the Choir* (Alces Press,
    1997) and appeared in *Cannon Fodder* magazine in 1998.
    © Christopher Twigg 1997

.. **Acknowledgements**

The biography of Christopher Twigg by Tom Lubbock first
appeared in the introduction to *In the Choir* (Alces Press,
1997) © Tom Lubbock 1997

'To The Round Moon' first appeared in *Adventures in the West*
(RMG, 1994). © Christopher Twigg 1994

'To My Feet' first appeared in *In The Choir* (Alces Press, 1997),
was broadcast as part of Channel 4's LITPOP series in 1998,
and appeared in APE Magazine. © Christopher Twigg 1997

'And Too Many Byrds' Records' © Tim Wells 1999

'Beautiful Girl Walks Out Of The Bar' and 'Up Down' © Andy
White 1999

'Her News' © Hugo Williams 1999

'Hello Sir': words and music by Robert Peter Williams. © 1997,
reproduced by permission of EMI Virgin Music Ltd,
London WC2H 0EH.

'Advising A Philistine' and 'One Down' © Kevin Williamson 1999

'Word Experience' and 'Volleying The Invisible' © Andy
Willoughby 1999

'A Prologue To History' first appeared on the twelve inch vinyl
'If You Tolerate This, Your Children Will be Next'.
Written by Nick Jones, Courtesy of Sony Music Publishing.
© Sony Music 1998

'My Little Empire' is taken from the album *This is my Truth*,
1998. Written by Nick Jones, Courtesy of Sony Music
Publishing. © Sony Music 1998

'The Life & Death Of Art' and 'The Cyber Tragedy' first
appeared in *Casual Sex and Other Verse* (Bantam Books,
1997). © Murray Lachlan Young 1997

'Cybersex' first appeared in *Propa Propaganda* (Bloodaxe Books,
1996). © Benjamin Zephaniah 1996